CW00548627

POETS IN BLOOM 2004

Edited by

Sarah Marshall

To one of the most
  beautiful people I've met
on   my short time on this
planet,
    keep the faith
    live it like you
      love it

  You will always be an

  Inspiration

      love and respect
        always
                Mark

First published in Great Britain in 2004 by
POETRY NOW
Remus House,
Coltsfoot Drive,
Peterborough, PE2 9JX
Telephone (01733) 898101
Fax (01733) 313524

SB ISBN 1 84460 830 1

FOREWORD

Although we are a nation of poets we are accused of not reading poetry, or buying poetry books. After many years of listening to the incessant gripes of poetry publishers, I can only assume that the books they publish, in general, are books that most people do not want to read.

Poetry should not be obscure, introverted, and as cryptic as a crossword puzzle: it is the poet's duty to reach out and embrace the world.

The world owes the poet nothing and we should not be expected to dig and delve into a rambling discourse searching for some inner meaning.

The reason we write poetry (and almost all of us do) is because we want to communicate: an ideal; an idea; or a specific feeling. Poetry is as essential in communication, as a letter; a radio; a telephone, and the main criterion for selecting the poems in this anthology is very simple: they communicate.

CONTENTS

Find The Answer In Your Heart	Sofia Pernikis	1
Bentham - God's Garden	Jeannie Ashplant	2
Miss Pink Leaf	Adhel Azad	3
The Drive	Mary Hunter	4
The Red Squirrel	Geraldine S Stephenson	5
Autumn's Treasure Chest	Valerie Perry	6
Seed Time Feed Time	Linda Collins	7
Friends, In Need	Dave Kwiatkowski	8
Season Struggles	Lewis Ewers	9
Spring	Trudy Valentine	10
Poppy Fields	Sophie Peppercorn	11
Out In My Garden	Janet Hughes	12
Spoilt Spring	Malcolm Gregory Coleman	13
If Only	Jayne Hosmer	14
My Place	Grace Long	16
Inside Looking Out	Angela Cooney	17
Creation	Andrew Gradwell	18
Take Time	A Dormer	19
Rose Garden	Chris Barnes	20
Day Dreams	Beryl Shepard Leece	22
Nature Ramble	Lorraine Gallagher	23
The Garden	Sarah Seymour	24
Wicked As A Wasp	Kay Dawn Tonks	25
Nature's Gift -		
The Lake Of Grasmere	Zarqua Jamil	26
Our Earth	Carol Milner	27
Small Talk	Evelyn E Griffin	28
Autumn	Dorothy Fuller	29
Wild And Free	Rusty Broadspear	30
Glenda's Garden	Cecilia Hill	31
Night-Time	Nikohl Medley	32
Daisy	Ben Stone	33
Heavy Weather	Andrew Latham	34
The Field	Rosemary McBarron	35
The Bluebells Of The Dell	Stephen Brearley	36
Just Roaming	Jim Livermore	37

The Window Box	C Webster	38
Beauty	Barbara Wakefield	39
Love In The Borders	Sheila J Leheup	40
Easter Memories	Duncan S Cromar	41
The Swan's Song	Vikki Rimmer	42
The Shower	Peter Isgar	43
Kent College Roundabout	Patricia Adele Draper	44
Raindrops	Kyra Reynolds	45
Global Warming	Nick Marshall	46
Nature's Beauty	Sian Pooley	48
Human Nature	Amanda Stanley	49
Blackbirds In The Garden	G E Harrison	50
Rose	Craig Lyn-Cook	52
Splendid's Verse	James Spoors	53
Summer's Peak	C A Walsh	54
Wise Is The Oak	Sara Rhys	55
The Change	Pey Colborne	56
The Swiftness Of Time	Belinda Louise Summerfield	57
My Garden	Vivien Exall	58
Who Am I?	Leanne Mitchell	59
Dare!	A Quinn	60
Peace	Jean Ruddick	61
Summer Explosion	Mary Spence	62
The Garden Senses	J Hinson	63
The Bat	Moira Round	64
My Haven	Ann Marie Chapman	65
November	Angela Dolphin	66
North Sea	Rebecca	67
Untitled	Pauline Morrow	68
A Gardener's Poem	E V Bowles	69
Springtime	R C Durrant	70
Summer Dreams	S Short	71
Winning A Woman	Paul B Shipley	72
Numb	Nicole Bushe	73
The Parrot Nation	Eric McCrossan	74
A Garden	J E Davies	75
Bird Song	Steve Ray Knight	76
Waves	Karen Louise Allen	77

Nature's Twist	Maria Stewart	78
Springtime	Mariè Brown	79
My Garden	Chris McLeod	80
Gardening	Gwynfa Evans	81
In The Garden	K Brown	82
In The Garden	Claire O'Sullivan	83
The Cuckoo	J H Christie	84
A Violet	Patricia Treherne	85
Aphrodite's Legacy	Maria Germaine	86
Stand Back And Admire!	Elsa Beggs	87
How Now Brown Cow	John A Duffy	88
Free	Stan Darby	89
Mother Nature's Countryside	Peter Bayliss	90
Locked In A Classroom On A Summer's Day	Summer Lili	91
Seasonal Wonders	Sue Hetherington	92
No It In Autumn	Lily Carmen Pepper	93
Little Leaf	Daniel Ambrose	94
Nature Smiles	Margaret Taylor	95
Road Runner	A Mayne	96
The Witches' Wishing Well	Carly Dugmore	97
The Never-Ending Saga	Stan Kay-Walton	98
Spring (Peresephone)	M P Johnson	99
When Summer Comes	Frank Thomas	100
Secrets Of The Sea	Rita Algar	101
Spring Time	Amanda Baldwin	102
Labour Of Love	Karen M Green	103
Enjoy Your Weeds	Kenneth Berry	104
The Sensory Garden	B M Beatson	105
In The Country	Lilian Florence Jones	106
Untitled	Marq Sutton	107
My Garden	Marilyn Pullan	108
Eagle Owl	Michael Kelly	110
Spring	Harry Miller	111
Seasons	Janet Mears	112
God's New City	Vi Berriff	113
A Midsummer Night's Dream	Bethany Jones	114
All Seasons	I Lee	115

The Garden	J T Hazell	116
A Sunny Day In 1932	Edna Kitchen	117
Care Of Our Countryside	J Jones	118
In My Garden	Lynne Clements	120
It Had To Go	John Simpson	121
Duty Bound	G J Hancock	122
Serenity	P Cannon	123
The Sunflower	Dorothy Haywood	124
Flower	Lauren Angela Curley	125
The Garden	Frances Rankine	126
Flowers	M Perkins	127
Seasons Four	Arthur T Blakemore	128
Spring	A Roach	129
Victoria's Walls	Sean Kinsella	130
A Winter Garden	Trish Lomas	131
The Squirrel	Sharon Howells	132
The Hedgehog's Lament	Patricia Jennings	133
The Sounds Of Spring	M Hooton	134
A Foxy Tale	Ronald H Blee	135
Ladybird	Louise Mortimer	136
The Willow Cottage	Nina	137
My Garden	Rhoda D Ribbens	138
Sparrows Pond	Daniel Miles	139
Whispering	April Dickinson-Owen	140
Seeds For Tomorrow	Linda Kettle	141
4 Seasons	Jane Abbott	142
Thor!	Cliff Holt	143
Stop, Look And Listen	Doug Downton	144
Spring	Dee Degnan	146
Thixendale	Sara Ward	147
My Four-Legged Friend	H Griffiths	148
Seasons	Wilhelm	149
Did You See That?	Sheila Neary	150
Garden Rhythm	Lucy Holloway	151
My Prize Beauty	Barbara Senior	152
Love, Spring's Eternal Toil	Len Simms	153
Stormy Weather	Kareen Smith	154
Spring	Doris Richards	155

Awakening	Valerie Mellor	156
The Fox	B P Willetts	157
Sheep	Simon Zonenblick	158
Green	Gael Nash	159
Woods Of The Ancient Ones	Josephine Carter	160
Gazebos In Gardens	Elizabeth Hunter	161
Butterfly	Kathleen McCarthy	162
Gypsy Girl	Beryl Barlow	163
The World About Us	Sheila Waller	164
Kestrel, At Sunset	Chris White	165
Colours Of Monday	Sara Church	166
Untitled	Deana Sawyer	167
Garden Ghost	Conor McGreevy	168
Early Spring In The Park	Helen Dalgleish	169
Daydreams Of My English Rose	Keith Potter	170
Walled Garden	Alan J Morgan	171
Beyond The Breakers	Liz Jacques	172
Summer Is Almost Here	P Dowse	173
The Old Man	Hilary Ambrose	174
A New Beginning	Tina Butterworth	175
Welcome Spring	Teresa R Chester	176
Summer Loving	S Ballard	177
Weed Shall Surrender	Clare Stubbs	178
World From Nature's Window	Hayley Slade	179
We Are Strangers	Mekhled Al-zaza	180
The Scarecrow	Sue James	181
A Single Silent Flame	James I Robson	182

FIND THE ANSWERS IN YOUR HEART

Never know what the future brings,
Can you ask me about it, please?
I think I've got an answer for you,
Waiting for its time to be wanted at ease.

So you're ready for an answer,
That will open your heart to show you the beauty of life?
If so, come with me,
If wishing to experience your life and see it right here before your eyes.

Can you see that star shining in the sky?
The star that is miles away, but it's right here within your mind.
You can reach for it,
And if you really wish for it, you will find its light
Being born again, in your heart.

What is the word 'future'?
That ties everyone's tongues and minds in a knot, not letting go,
But equally not giving away its deepest secret,
That lies within anyone's reach, just seconds away,
But eternities to come and go.

Never know what the future brings,
Can you ask me about it, please?
I thought I've got an answer for you,
But realised, it's right here, it's with you.

Sofia Pernikis

BENTHAM - GOD'S GARDEN

Your birthday arrived once again
And to a church along a country lane
I bring my bright spring flowers
But am beaten by Mother Nature's powers

Through the gate I peer in awe
At the many snowdrops making a floor
To some this churchyard may be forsaken
Yet this land the flora and fauna have retaken

Rabbits have made this place their home
And by night fox, mole and badger roam
Amongst the buttercups they play and graze
Observed on high only by God's gaze

Now a perfect place of peace
In this Eden to which God holds the lease
I'll leave you silently sleeping
Knowing you're in the Lord's safe keeping.

Jeannie Ashplant

MISS PINK LEAF

Trees with pink leaves
- pretty like many,
sky with pixel blue clarity
- captivating and
the grass dotted by little yellows
- delectable,
what turns my head
and burns my eyes
- is the burning sun
and gentle whispers
- of the easterly breeze
this is what this season brings.

It makes you stay out till late,
forgetful of time
is the season of play.

Laying on the grass
of little yellows.

Softly enjoying
Miss Pink.

Adhel Azad

THE DRIVE

I walk into the silent drive
I blink, and it comes alive
The trees moan and sway in the sun
The squirrels scurry up into them

The birds are flapping in the breeze
The others hurry into the leaves
The hare darts into the woods

The guinea fowl wander past
Wondering if their next snack will be in the grass
The deer give you an almighty glare
As Peter the peacock
Struts his stuff
Looking for some tasty stuff.

Mary Hunter

THE RED SQUIRREL

Their coats are red with bushy tail
To keep them warm from winter's gale,
Their tummies have a coat of white
To see them is a real delight.

With big, bright eyes and tufted ears
They forage until food appears,
From where they buried nuts away
To eat them on a winter's day.

You see their nose and whiskers twitch
They scratch a most annoying itch,
With their long claws so razor sharp
They climb the trees and cling to bark.

A squirrel proves itself most able
Finding a meal from a bird table
On peanuts you see that they're no clown
And munch from feeders upside down.

In spring young squirrels like to play
They follow Mum out from their dray
Exploring everything outside
Not straying far from Mother's side

It's great to see them feed and play
Staying close throughout the day
Investigating all they see
Learning their skills on branch and tree.

In weeks and months they soon grow
Young squirrels learn what they must know
To scale the treetops fearlessly
Surviving life on land and tree.

Geraldine S Stephenson

AUTUMN'S TREASURE CHEST

Autumn has opened the lid of her treasure chest,
Revealing the bounty kept hidden inside -
Gold from the cornfields, as it fell to the reaper.
Dewdrops like diamonds that sparkle and shine,
And in the garden, where flowers are growing
Amethyst and garnet reign supreme in the beds,
Deep ruby and topaz the leaves now are turning
And berries in hedgerows in all shades of red.

Emerald green still covers the hillsides,
Mixed with violet and sapphire; colours you least would expect.
And the sunsets, like opals are a mixture of colours
Fiery one moment, and cool crystal the next -
An ivory rose 'gainst the wall in the garden
Is gilded with gold dust by the sun's weakening rays.
And the amber of beechnuts, collected by squirrels
As food for the winter, when they sleep in their dreys.

Early frosts, silver the grass in the morning, turquoise and jade
Shadows 'neath the trees can be seen.
A sheen like a pearl paints the fruit in the orchard
And decorates the trees where the spider has been.
These are the riches, the gems of the autumn;
Each year on show as the harvest comes home.
Then the lid gently closes, before Brother Winter,
Arrives in his season with jewels of his own . . .

Valerie Perry

SEED TIME FEED TIME

Beans, carrots, flowers and chives
Tasty greens on juicy vines.
I watch them come on a quiet day
Time doesn't matter, if night or day.
I've worked so hard on my garden plot
To be soul destroyed by this furry lot!
Rabbit, rabbit, rabbit
Is all the family hear
Mum's getting cross as they've munched her plot
Then comes the deer, finding tender shoots
Bark on the fruit tree
Leaves on a shrub
He doesn't care what he has for tea.
Even curry plant and rosemary.
I watch them all with sheer delight,
But each year I know
I'm in the same old plight.
Wire fencing's a price, as I've discovered
So I'll continue to watch
As my hard work's in vain
And enjoy all the pleasures
Of my garden's gain.

Linda Collins

FRIENDS, IN NEED

Look after your environment
And it will look after you
Our heritage, is our legacy
Our countryside's and gardens too.
Ducks and swans, on a glistening pond
Drift by . . . on a lazy summer day
Wildlife . . . at its most beautiful
We shouldn't get in their way.
They are here for our pleasure
Because God . . . put them there
They are an English treasure
So let us show we care.
These creatures needn't be hurt
The creatures needn't die
So don't pollute their waters
It's a crime . . . is the reason why.
Foxes and hedgehogs
Creatures of the night
Simply searching for survival food
Don't hinder their plight.
They have families . . . just like us
And want them to survive
So don't let them die, under wheels of a car
Keep nature's friends alive.
Squirrels, birds, geese and herds
Farmlands . . . and cities too
We have to look after, what we have left
Now it's all up to you.

Dave Kwiatkowski

SEASON STRUGGLES

Howling winds run down the lane
To rustle the hair of the horse's mane,
To clean the path of the dying leaves
That have fallen from the sleepy trees.

Once blossom grew, coloured and bright
But now its splendour has gone from sight,
Old Man Winter lays down his frost
And summer's flowers are once more lost.

Miss Spring's blue skies bring hope for life
And Winter fails to bring his strife,
Tight buds grow quick on cut down stems
Dew covered grass shine bright like gems.

Mother Nature is at her best
Old Man Winter, asleep in rest,
Summer has an all night party
But Winter will not be so hearty.

Lewis Ewers (12)

SPRING

Get up
Get up
Oh for spring's sake
Please get up
Come on
Let's skip over warm winter puddles
And hum with the bees in the trees
Get up
And just look at this morning
Get up
For spring's sake please.

Trudy Valentine

POPPY FIELDS

Red amongst the bright corn fields,
Swinging gently to and fro.

As cold winds come,
They hang their heads,
Scatter their seeds,
But brighten up the day.

Red amongst the bright corn fields,
Swinging gently to and fro.

They lighten up the gloomy skies,
Saying, 'Stop a little while . . .
To share my vibrant red smile.'

Red amongst the bright corn fields,
Swinging gently to and fro.

Sophie Peppercorn (13)

OUT IN MY GARDEN

Out in my garden
The lawn is overgrown,
The border needs digging
As seeds need to be sown.
Out in my garden
There's such a lot to do,
Where do I begin?
I just haven't got a clue.
Out in my garden
Using blood, sweat and toil,
It takes such a lot
To be at one with the soil.
Out in my garden
Which is overgrown with weeds,
I must eradicate them
Before I sow the seeds.
Out in my garden
Armed with fork, spade and hoe,
It's time to get cracking
So it's off to work we go.
Out in my garden
Now there is plenty of room,
For the seeds to flourish
And the flowers to bloom.

Janet Hughes

SPOILT SPRING

The magma of anger welled up from my bowels
Past my chest and then entered my throat,
And my face it grew red from the fury I felt
As I saw what man's debris had done to the moat.

The lovely old castle with its nearby wood
With bluebells and creatures wild and free,
Which have graced this land for many a day
Now spoiled by man's discarded technology.

Malcolm Gregory Coleman

IF ONLY

I wish I were a gardener
As I do not have a clue
Today I aim to try it
Let's see what I can do

First I start to do my lawn
My mower blades soon break
I knew before I started
This would be a big mistake

I am sure to be a gardener
You need a City & Guilds
My buttercups and daisies
Should be in the fields

I attempt to trim my hedges
They end up full of gaps
As I was constantly bombarded
By groups of nasty gnats

I've now upset the wasp nest
Argh! I've just been stung
I'm flapping round my garden
Not my idea of fun

Time to try some weeding
Or are they flowers that are dead?
I think I next will have concussion
Fruits from my apple tree, are falling on my head

While trying to prune the roses
I'm sore, arms cut to shreds
So I carefully plant some seeds in,
Create a flowerbed

Think it's time to stop now
But there's still so much to do
Time to make that phone call
To Ground Force and the crew.

Jayne Hosmer

MY PLACE

The beach is a place just for me,
Where my thoughts can change like
The soul of the sea.
I can sit on the sand and contemplate,
All my thoughts and sorrowful state.

Watching the rolling back and forth of the tide,
Nothing in my mind is able to hide.
Just like debris washed onto the shore,
All my thoughts come out of store.

The beach is a place just for me,
Where my mind gets emptied, I'm finally free.
I can finally mull over every tiny detail,
All by myself I can sort out my trail.

The serenity makes my heart so at ease,
My mind is at peace from the
Tranquil sound of the sea.
It is so atmospheric, it takes my breath away,
So I ponder my thoughts, here I wish to stay.

Grace Long

INSIDE LOOKING OUT

End of January into February my garden is lacking in bloom
Empty pots and baskets look full of gloom,
The grass is lank and patchy with no volume
The holly bush with no berries or vroom,
Sunshine creeps through to my outdoor room
Snowdrops are almost about to illume,
So we can definitely assume
Spring is on its way to give off a special perfume,
How wonderful the seasonal change does loom
Almost time to get out there with the tools and broom,
Preparing seeds and soil to dress up my garden in a colourful costume.

Angela Cooney

CREATION

Great coat flapping,
Nailed boots stamping,
Singing, muttering under breath.
Rough hands weeding,
Digging, seeding
Giving life and giving death.
The gardener towers,
Over flowers.
Head lost in blue and summer sun.
Tired and aching,
Stiff fingers shaking,
He rests and smiles on all he's done.

Andrew Gradwell

TAKE TIME

Take time to view the sunrise,
Witness the start of day,
Watch the sun climb in the heavens
And dispel the night away.
Take time to watch it meander
Across the bright blue sky,
See it reach its zenith
And then begin its descent.
Watch the shadows lengthen,
A spectacular event.
Take time and enjoy the sunset
At the closing of the day,
The bright red orange glow
Will surely light the way.
The light gives way to darkness
The moon begins its glow,
The stars shine in the heavens
And begins a brand new show.
It seems that all too often,
In this life's too rapid pace,
We don't take time to see.
And like all the good Lord's works
The spectacle is free.

A Dormer

ROSE GARDEN

Nurtured from the juice of Mother Earth
you begin life with tender bud free stems
and slender featureless unattractive stalks,
with soft pimple-like featureless thorns
and virgin sap that makes its random walk.

Time passes by and soon you yield fleshier budded stems;
curvier, luscious, teasing, tempting stalks;
barbed aerial plastic thorns which, while still virginal,
capably drew first blood upon, unsuspecting, uninvited touch.

You quickly mature to gain firm sweet succulent buds
upon those tantalising stems and swollen stalks;
as unashamedly you taste soft, subtle summer's rain
erotically tonguing your cupped greenery.

Fresh, young greenery sustained by moist caress
such in intimate response you thrust up and open your living bouquet
of full size blooms, some like ruby red pouting lips,
some soft and pink like a blushing bride's cheek,
others purest white like her veil.

I walk through your midst and take deep breaths
admiring your feminine scent. Heaven sent, heavy, powdery scent
that wafts on the gentle warming breezes
and relaxes my mind and I dream of Hawaii or an Arab bazaar.

Yet all too soon I fear first petals will blow
from those knowing stems, your woody, weathered stalks
and battered droopy thorns being firmly grasped
by late autumn's early morning chill,
which slows sap's meandering walk.

I dread the thought of all your petals lost,
and swelling hips upon your ageing stems,
and that notion of bent and battered thorns
only just jutting through winter's snows
clinging upon your gaited graying, knotted stalks;

Stalks brittle and snapping under a blanching death angel's load
and I pray and weep for your miraculous resurrection,
fresh turgidity for those soggy limp and lifeless thorns;
another spring; your former beauty once adorned, restored.

Chris Barnes

Day Dreams

Give me a summer's azure sky,
The joyous bird songs way up high.

Give me a meadow, fragrant sweet,
The buttercups beneath my feet.

Give me a path through woodland glade,
The arching trees, the rustic shade.

Give me a brook o'er weathered stones,
A winding way all overgrown.

Give me a cottage, mellowed old,
Whose thatch is part of England's wold.

Give me a garden's fragrant flowers,
To while away contented hours.

Give me a quaint old market town,
With cobbled ways to browse around.

Give me good Lord a heart to share
The beauty I find everywhere.

Beryl Shepard Leece

NATURE RAMBLE

A nature ramble's what I like
Up on a summer's day
To walk through fields and bushes
And to smell the new mown hay
To see sheep and cows a grazing
I simply find amazing
A hawk above me soaring high
Into the deepest bluest sky
It sees a tiny mouse below
And swoops to get it, there it goes
The fox that's running swiftly past
Is off to feed its family fast
The little ones will hungry get
If it's not home before sunset
I see the pheasant in the fields
A pretty sight to see
And what's that sound? A cuckoo
Above me in the trees
I really love the country
For hours I could roam
But it's nice when you have finished
To find your way back home.

Lorraine Gallagher

THE GARDEN

A gardener's day is never done,
Hoeing, weeding in the sun.
When it rains the weeds regrow
And the lawns require another mow.
Clusters of bulbs flowering in spring,
The robin sits on the fence and sings.
Butterflies float softly by,
Birds soaring above in the sky.
Flowers on plants, leaves on trees,
Buzzing about gnats, wasps and bees.
The garden is an orchestra of chaos and sound,
Many species are there to be found.
The satisfaction of the work
And the view are all the perks.
The finished garden makes it all worthwhile,
Creating your own individual style.

Sarah Seymour

WICKED AS A WASP

Hey something's started to bother me,
As I work, on my PC,
One minute happy, just sitting here,
Then all of a sudden, froze with fear.

A loud noise, I detect nearby,
Is it a wasp, a bee or a fly,
No I was right, the very first time
A nasty great wasp, making a b-line.

As I sit here, paralysed and numb,
Oh no, it's landed, on my bum,
Do I run, or do I stay,
Or pray to God, it'll go away.

No it's not shifting, not one inch,
Oh no I can feel, a painful pinch,
Yes it's got me, right on the cheek,
Now I'm not able, to sit down for a week.

Kay Dawn Tonks

NATURE'S GIFT - THE LAKE OF GRASMERE

Whilst upon my travels,
Lost in thought and garbed in a wanderer's robe
I sought a place of eternal peace
Where I could safely rest my soul.

By the command of Heaven, a wonder occurred
For at last my wish was heard
The sign of which was revealed anew,
When the unity of Heaven's precious cloud
Became the form of lovers, two.

When camaraderie sought a shoulder, new,
The sun of light affixed his stare
And there before my eyes emerged
The lake of Grasmere.

Humbled by the sight I saw
A resting place I found
And paid homage to the poet's quill
That drunk from the waters of Cumbria's crown.

Words of wisdom sought a friend
And a confidant blessed with tender voice,
A silent soul he found at last
Whose worth was a thousand fold.

Nature found a trusted love
And the beloved found a home
And together they built an abode of words
Where eloquence donned her golden gown.

Daffodils adorn her paths with gold
And her maiden soul dances as gentle breeze
Teasing and caressing wisdom's buds
Hidden deep within nature's ease.

Zarqua Jamil

OUR EARTH

If peace and harmony is what you are looking for
Then turn not to the sky, or by the seashore
Go back to nature, the plants in the ground
From the first snowdrops, daffodils and crocus
There is a riot of colour to be found
And as the nights get shorter, the days grow longer
The bees start to buzz and the birds to sing
To find spring has arrived is a wonderful thing
As you saw tiny seeds, life starts afresh
Snug and warm in their pots, like birds in their nest
Soon a bud appears, a leaf, a shoot
And under the soil, healthy long roots.
Soon out in your garden they will go
When summer comes, they will grow and grow.
From Asters to Wallflowers, the choice is yours
With their colour and scent, who wants to be indoors?
The sun on your back, the breeze in your hair
Take time to relax, just sit and stare
At Mother Nature in all her glory,
Every living thing is part of her story.
And as time passes through the seasons
Each new day, a different reason
For life on our planet, our wonderful Earth
But it's up to all of us, everyone,
To care for her with all we are worth.

Carol Milner

SMALL TALK

A buttercup was heard to say
To a daisy by her side
'Don't you think this is,
A rather nice place to reside?
And I keep this little corner
Really very bright,'
'A patch of gold,' the daisy said
'Of course you are so right.'

They often talk together,
And discuss things like the weather
And whether they fulfil
The garden's needs,
But when the robin is about
There is not the slightest doubt,
He will tell them, 'they are wild flowers
And not weeds.'

Evelyn E Griffin

AUTUMN

Autumn leaves come tumbling down
Some are yellow, some are brown.
Swirling, twirling, edges curling
Marvellous colours, all unfurling.
Greens and reds, with streaks of yellow
Oak leaves, brown, old and mellow.
The wind blows them round and round
Into heaps upon the ground.
Then picks them up and swirls them high
Up into the cloudy sky.
As you walk along the lane
Leaves come swirling round again.
Tramp through piles, feet a munching
Lovely sounds of feet a crunching.
Autumn is a lovely season
Nature changes without reason.
Surely now that winter's coming
There will be no bees a humming.
No birds can shelter in the trees
Shelter from the winter's breeze.
Branches bare, no leaves remain
Until the spring comes round again.

Dorothy Fuller

WILD AND FREE

Like strands of beautiful black silk, the dark rain
Delicately dripped from the foliage,
Giving off a wild sweet perfume.
As the orange ball of fire dipped dramatically,
An eerie glow capped the treetops,
Tomorrow was entering nature's womb.
Wildlife cackling, far away, in the distant hills.
I stood still, aware of possible predators,
But all was clear, my mind took me home.
A six month courtship with nature, was all I'd had,
But it was serious and would last forever,
Here I would stay and live and roam.
Home was thousands of miles and years away,
A foreign city that never sleeps,
With people and money, never lies still.
I see a pond with a shroud of evening mist
Through which clouds of insects dart
On the evening air, their chattering so shrill.
Every turn that nature takes is so wonderful,
I decide to lay my head,
And let this wondrous union lead me to sleep.
I dream that we are as one with the universe,
And that everything I see is a source of light.
A dream to remember and forever to keep.

Rusty Broadspear

GLENDA'S GARDEN

I was awakened by a symphony of sounds
Like a drum beat raining down
Rapping on my head, calling for my attention
Heavy eyelids lifted like curtains from the stage to a
Paraphernalia of ferns and palms swaying in the breeze.

Once my senses had become attuned
To the darkened room
It wasn't long before the drumbeat was no rain
But a chorus of frogs, as if welcoming the train
My head ached no longer, but gladly listened to the throng
For it became a pleasant song.

With every pulsating croaking beat
The buzz of the insects would suddenly flow, like a rushing stream
Fingers of the palms rustled plucking at the harp strings
The breeze wafted through the window brushing my brow
Enticing the chimes to jangle in a swaying pace
And a cricket would chip-in to break the grace.

The croaking beat swung like a pendulum
Eating away the night to bring a wonderful sight
Like a reaper cutting his corn with one swift blow
Stemming the flow!
Only the cricket quenched its thirst
On the echoing bark stabbing at the dark.

The stage was set for the finale
The birds moved into the auditorium
Kookaburras chuckling, lorikeets chattering
Then hisses like a giant snake reverberating
Wings of the birds flapping
Like the palms, giving a standing ovation!

Cecilia Hill

NIGHT-TIME

As she stands there laughing, with such joy in her heart,
she notices it's time for the day to depart.
The sun bows gracefully, stars dance with glee,
night-time has come for you and me.
It offers lovers, time to become one,
it offers children dread, bedtime has come.
The birds no longer chirp or sing,
as they tuck their heads under their wing.
The flowers close their petals as darkness draws near,
in anticipation for morning to appear.
Crickets waking, ready for their song to be heard,
if you listen very closely, their chorus can be heard.
Black cats prowling in search of a mouse,
just a tasty morsel to taste in their mouth.
Spiders busily remaking their webs,
as morning draws near, their young to be fed.
The stars shining brightly with all their might,
soon will be the time for them to say goodnight.
With purples and pinks, dawn starts to appear,
black cats and spiders their sleep time is near.
Crickets ending their chorus, as they bow in farewell,
that night, they knew their songs did well.
The petals of flowers which were once so tight,
the morning dew opens them up so bright.
The birds awaking, with fresh song in mind,
over the horizon the sun we shall find.

Nikohl Medley

DAISY

A Stonehenge of
butterfly wings
a minute aircraft carrier
in a sea of green
swaying playing in the breeze
staring at the sky laying next to
me
your fragile life could pass us by
but only if we shut our eyes.

Ben Stone

HEAVY WEATHER

Now the sun has gone
We enter heavy weather
Battered by the squalls of your moods
Heavy weather,
Got to pull through
Heavy weather,
The weather of you.

Andrew Latham

THE FIELD

Cool, damp, early morning mists
twittering birds amidst budding trees
and lime green leaves
a field of buttercups
cowslip in the borders
sweet smelling May
a fracas of dogs in the distance
solitude of a landscape
sweeping up to hills
droplets of rain then refrain
breach a mound and all around
dandelion clocks with one eyed faces
watching, watching
dog runs, dives, splashes
into a rain filled dip, delighted
well worn tracks across the field
muddy turnstiles
blossom and blackbirds
promises of renewal
spring is, the best time.

Rosemary McBarron

THE BLUEBELLS OF THE DELL

Softly, silently, almost by surprise
The Dell is clothed in a beautiful blue
To compliment the skies.
No one knows who put them there
Just nature and it won't tell
From where they come and to where they go
The bluebells of the Dell.

They have so many uses
The bluebells of the Dell
For there exists a fairyland that children know quite well
Adult, adults, cannot see, for they have lost this view
Some bells being used as buckets to catch the morning dew.

Others make a lovely seat, and some a pretty hat
Whilst others act as doorbells, to warn mouse of the cat.
A fairy shakes a bluebell stem, it's bells laden with dew
So it can have a shower just like me and you
A world exists within a world, so try to get in touch
For once you cannot see these things
You miss so very much.

Some of the fairies build a grass church
With on top, a leafy tower
Inside of which they put bluebells
And chime them every hour.
They skip, they play, and laugh away, for them the time just flies
Until the evening shadows, steal across the skies
They are full of happy tiredness now, as anyone could tell
And so they all lay down to sleep
Midst the bluebells of the Dell.

Stephen Brearley

JUST ROAMING

How pleasant as a boy to roam the green fields,
Then, with others, to the woods, climb a safe tree.
Perhaps a little jealous, watch others braver than me,
Who climb higher than I could ever hope or wish.
Then wandering through the dense bushes and long grass,
Then, just to feel safe, calling out to each other,
Being relieved to get a happy reply from the other side.
Meeting at the end of this small happy adventure.
Then to go on to somewhere else, not too far away.
Boys and girls alike, all eager to be out and about.
The sunshine, which always seemed to be there,
Made each day, I cannot remember it raining, happy.
Another adventure, feats of daring, perhaps swank,
Being dared to do something not within your limits,
To fail dismally, to the happy banter of others.
Each of us doing those childish things of then.
A squabble, not serious, soon settled, play on.
Those halcyon days of my childhood of long ago.
Alas, now gone, but, I still have my happy thoughts.

Jim Livermore

THE WINDOW BOX

There's a window box outside our pub
Next to the sign saying we sell grub
It looks a bit tatty with its flaking paint
Yet beneath the bow window it should look quaint.

The trouble is it's so easy for dumping things
Like cigarette buts and beer can rings
There's a crisp packet too, and a glass of Coke
Upon which a dead wasp silently floats,

It is watered regularly, but with lager and beer
Could we have an alcoholic window box here?
But let's be honest and call a spade a spade.
It's just another dump that man has made.

Yet come what may in the early spring
When winter has fled and birds start to sing.
The earth in our window box is warmed by the sun
And little green shoots appear, one by one.

Then as if ordained by one of nature's peers,
The wind blows hard and the debris clears,
Then snowdrops appear, and crocuses too
Later the daffodils and hyacinths blue.

Some geraniums too have survived winter's bite
Now our window looks such a wonderful sight.
Later, on the patio, as the customers swig their beer
'Nice window box landlord' comes a voice loud and clear
'Yes' says the landlord, and he gives a little smirk.
'Takes a lot of looking after, but it's worth the hard work.'

C Webster

BEAUTY

Butterflies, butterflies
How pleasing to the eyes
So beautiful and sensitive
As they weave their magic and
Their way through the sky

Gliding swallow trails
Darting skippers
Graceful mourning cloaks
All need the sun
To help them fly

The life cycle of a butterfly
Is not very long
Till all at once
They are gone

Colourful and tiny
Harmless and frail
Just look for
Them along your trail

Their bed is under a leaf
To dance away from beneath
They need the sun
To make them fly
Up into the sky

Barbara Wakefield

LOVE IN THE BORDERS

Basil pined for Rosemary, growing in a pot
He cast her loving glances, and cried 'forget-me-not'
Now she was quite flirtatious, her eyes would often stray
To where her love, sweet William, grew just across the way

Poor William loved another, who shared his flowerbed
A haughty, black-eyed Susan of whom it must be said
She scorned her ardent lover, she wouldn't spare him thyme
No Canterbury bells would ring, no union sublime

So William sought another to ease his aching heart
He spied an amaranthus, then felt a Cupid's dart
And so like snow in summer, he melted at the sight
Of tearful love lies bleeding, the source of his delight

Now Rosemary was jealous, determined to try harder
Perhaps a red hot poker might dampen down his ardour
Love that's unrequited will evermore exist
Then feelings that are clouded become love in a mist.

Sheila J Leheup

EASTER MEMORIES

Many years ago when I was a young lad,
I think of the Easter's that we had,
The hens they really had to toil,
To supply the eggs for us to boil.

Into the hot water they were put,
Sometimes a kettle without a spout,
Really hard they were boiled,
Some of them often spoiled.

We painted them with home-made dyes,
All the colours of the skies,
Some had faces round and lumpy,
Others looked like Humpty Dumpty.

Then out to the open we all went,
Down the hill the eggs were sent,
How we shouted out with glee,
Some of them had hit a tree.

Then we picked off all the shells,
To see that underneath was well,
What was left was ours to eat,
Oh what fun, oh what a treat.

But these good times did not last,
Hard-boiled eggs now in the past,
Chocolate ones in every size,
So it's them I criticise.

So bring me back my childhood ways,
When kids enjoyed their Easter days,
It's something I would love to see,
But all I have is memories.

Duncan S Cromar

THE SWAN'S SONG

It's only going to get harder,
Now spring is here everything wakes,
But you.

Battered by winter winds was comfort,
Physical pain matched that within,
Without you.

Empty feelings aren't numb, they hurt,
Longing washes at my heart,
Losing you.

Forever gliding from my own reflection
Unable to escape the watery mirror,
Just me.

Saw two entwined, like we once were,
Swimming together by the shore, thought
Only of you.

I dream of stroking your neck,
Our faces meet in heart-shaped love -
Awoke alone.

Unable to move on or live here alone
Twosome's what made us whole
Me and you.

Vikki Rimmer

THE SHOWER

The creaking pines of the forest sway
As the gentle breeze begins to play,
Its mesmeric pull continues to tease
And tickle branches of graceful trees.

The giggling ferns are shuffling below
For a ringside seat to watch the show.
Bustling and rustling they try to settle
Pushing aside the coarse stinging nettle.

Pine cones are falling across the floor
A gracious offering to feed their poor.
While busy squirrels nervously scratch
Wide-eyed and alert, guarding their patch.

Then silence falls, no breath is heard
No chattering chicks, no humming bird.
Tension mounts with unbearable hush
Above the trees the clouds do rush.

The first arrive with a tender caress,
Small explosions that conquer stress.
The tiny ferns give a thankful bow
As each drop falls to wet their brow.

Silence is shattered by a thunderous roar
A million raindrops hit the forest floor.
A rousing symphony, with volume raised
The bluebells cowering battered and dazed.

Then sunlight breaks through the trees
And raindrops sparkle like crystal beads.
The grateful forest can rest once more
It's life force flowing through every pore.

Peter Isgar

KENT COLLEGE ROUNDABOUT

By Kent College, in Chatham,
There's a roundabout that's always green.
Whatever the season of the year,
There's a picture to be seen.
In summer it's mainly green,
With white daisies dotted here and there,
And the autumn leaves are lovely,
But in spring it is most fair.

Before the snow has melted
The sweet crocuses come bursting through.
They smile midst the white, snowy blanket,
Arrayed in colourful hue.
After these come the daffodils,
Standing tall, with their sleepy heads.
Of delicate cream and vibrant gold,
Rise up from their earthy beds.

Even straighter, like soldiers,
Ramrod tall, glorious tulips bold,
Their vivid colours burn the senses,
Battle dress of red and gold.
And dancing around their feet,
Humble dandelions and buttercups.
Joy to the striped, clumsy bumblebee,
As their sweet nectar he sups.

When I pass that roundabout
I give thanks to those gardeners of old,
Who planted bulbs with such loving care,
For travellers to behold.
Time capsule of the seasons,
Nature's calendar all wrapped in one.
Mowed by the council, watered by rain
And blessed by the smiling sun.

Patricia Adele Draper

RAINDROPS

A golden shaft splits,
Hangs suspended.
Sparkles caught in a waltz.
Tidal waves rush through the calm,
Destroying tiny cities.
The colony broken.
All run for cover
Amid a shimmer of
Raindrops.

Kyra Reynolds

GLOBAL WARMING
(This poem was inspired by an overheard conversation between a barman and a Yorkshire man)

What is this global warming,
and will it really hurt?
Or does it just mean,
I can roll the sleeves up on m' shirt?

What is this global warming,
this greenhouse affect?
A hole in the ozone,
what will they think of next?

What is this global warming,
caused by aerosol gases?
All that harm from one small can,
their talking out their arses.

What is this global warming?
Why shouldn't I start m' car?
I'm going to the pub,
I know it ain't that far.

What is this global warming,
the cars are at a standstill?
Well cut a road through that green field,
a tunnel through that hill.

What is this global warming?
The trees add summut t'air?
I see a tree, a waste of space,
I couldn't even care.

What is this global warming?
The icecaps are melting,
The sea level's rising
But Blackpool, we're sweltering!

What is this global warming,
they all keep chunnering about?
Got a wife and seven kids,
spot a sun, couldn't do without.

What is this global warming?
Bloody lucky for some,
I'm back at home at Barnsley,
and it's pissing down again.

What is this global warming,
that's messing up our lives?
I can't see, hear, or touch it,
I think it's a pack of lies.

What is this global warming?
I'm getting rather bored.
So pull another pint barman,
And I wunna say another word . . .

Nick Marshall

NATURE'S BEAUTY

Why are these pearls flowing from my eyes?
Why is there a blissful feeling within my heart?
What is this supple experience I can feel?
What else could this be?
But nature at her best
Granting me the beauty of her soul

The wild horse gallops free
The spirited hawk glides limitless
The kind-hearted deer trots along
What else could this be?
But nature at her best
Granting freedom to her children

The people come and the people go
They don't see her soul
They don't listen to her heart
They miss her true beauty
They miss her true freedom
They miss nature at her best

The trees come alive with the sound of life
The flowers are scented and bright
The grass is lush and green
What else could this be?
But nature at her best
And now she is ready to share her world with us.

Sian Pooley

HUMAN NATURE

For what do we claim providence in our daily affairs?
As the humdrum complaisance of life unfurls,
For human nature is neither without fault nor is it fail-safe,
Even the calmest waters have their undercurrent.

All beauty is malleable; patience is a maelstrom of endurance,
Temperance is a virtue of angels and saints,
Sin is a commonplace reality,
Thus, why must we fear certain truth?

No conscience is safe from the talons of doubt,
Nor the stranglehold of uncertainty and regret,
As the questions of time reach out toward the sun,
Enlightenment is born of the darkness.

Only in the blackness of souls can we see ourselves,
Only in the valley of our fears do we truly speak,
That which we attain from trail and error,
May be all we shall ever know of life.

There is an ill wind blowing through the foothills of reason,
Which entraps our secrets deep beneath our skin,
Unspoken words we long to voice,
Ever more fail to see the light of day.

But what is a man who has never lived?
He is a man; who has walked a trial of majestic nonchalance,
One; who has seldom fought for his sanity,
Nor gazed upon the threshold of sadness in hope.

From each broken stem a stronger branch will grow,
From each fallen seed a mighty tree,
Our weaknesses become that which make us strong,
And guide us through eternity beguiled.

Amanda Stanley

BLACKBIRDS IN THE GARDEN

A blackbird with its mate,
Flying high searching for bait,
A wriggling worm, a sunflower seed,
Whatever will provide a good feed!

They chase each other over the lawn,
Finding their food in the early dawn,
So clever are these delicate creatures,
Their many senses are amazing features!

They brave such inclement weathers
And simply, ruffle their sleek feathers!
They take shelter in the shrubs
And then, keep hunting for garden grubs!

Nesting is a special time
And nests are created in an established pine.
Eggs are laid and well protected
By the hen blackbird, not readily ejected!

The cock blackbird fetches and carries
Food for the hen, while she tarries.
A long time she will sit and wait
For her young to hatch, and take their first bait!

Their fledglings' survival will be a fight
And the hen will protect them with all her might.
The day comes when they can fly alone,
But, can always find their way home!

As time passes they learn how to feed
Independently, find worms and sunflower seeds.
How proud the hen and cock blackbirds must feel,
To see their fledglings close at heel!

Soon they will fly the nest,
Having done their very best
To live independently and survive,
So wonderful to be free and alive!

G E Harrison

ROSE

Let me hold you rose:
once more petals fall as
she blushes with red dimpled cheeks
waves breaking over my body
she coloured her hair sea for me.
Foam white trails along her sides

I will tread lightly upon her name
I will not crush her skin,
delicate little flower.
We dance heads clouded
hand in my hand, heart in my heart,
feet floating over polished crystal sea
tendrils barely touching my face.
Twirling on tiptoe we pass
I gazed careful not to sear
a thin thread between eyes
neat blue flames

Archer shoots his arrow and she falls,
concave curve, after concave curve
hand against the small of her back,
fluttering lightly to the ground
until she's a feathered puddle at my feet.

Craig Lyn-Cook

Splendid's Verse

I long to write proses
Of orchids and roses
And beautiful things of the wild
My life is beguiled
In the passing of time
I long to write poems that will rhyme.
I long to write verse that will stir up the blood
Of life and love and all things good
But I am lost in a forage of ideas
Accumulated over my years.
I must smell the flowers
That a fair heart devours
And hold a garden in my gaze
'Til the petals of primrose amaze.
There will always be charm
That pits its might against harm,
So God give me strength
To try at length
To write of nature as this precious making of yours
Before you take my hand through those doors.

James Spoors

SUMMER'S PEAK

Over the hills I wander through the trees over yonder,
I can see the birds and the bees in the sycamore trees,
and the hornbeam looking ever so splendid,
I walk down on the path where the river runs ever so fast,
and I duck as the dragonfly just flies by me.
I can see the farmhouse from where I stand,
it's ever so grand, it lifts my spirits no end,
to see my animal friends all around me.
I look down and see all the land around me,
and I think about thee with no garden.

For this is what God, gave to thee all ornamental,
free and colour so pure and gentle,
there's fruit on the trees and coloured leaves
so I'll just take a fruit that I fancy,
I open my eyes to find by surprise
that I'm back in my garden that's real fancy.
There's honeysuckle, ivy and clematis too,
I see the butterfly bush, broom and hosta too.
The magnolia, azalea and rhododendrons all stand out,
they look real nice without a doubt.

The trumpet vine and willow tree all look proud to be around thee.
So next time you look, look more deeply
and you will find real beauty all around thee.

C A Walsh

WISE IS THE OAK

Wise is the oak,
The king of the wood,
The lord of the forest,
If ever he could
Utter a word,
What would that word be?
And how might it sound?
Perhaps he can see,
If that be the case,
Which way would he gaze?
And what would he find,
As he witnesses days,
Come and go,
Day and night,
Drought and flood,
Dark and light,
He witnesses whether or not,
He has sight,
For this king may not,
Bear a crown made of gold,
No robes does he wear,
And he may grow old,
But ever the king of the wood,
Will he be,
For wise is the oak,
The most kingly tree.

Sara Rhys

THE CHANGE
(Winter to spring)

Blue winter days crack open,
Thin as eggshells of a hidden bird
In the hedgerows.

The lichens cling to the stone wall,
Above the valley,
Bald trees wave their hair of mist,
Ice wraps the berry, spikes of
Frost, sharper than thorn.

Wet, rich mint
Meadows alongside
Furrows of earth,
Loam and leaves.

The silent damp goes deep,
Holds you under in this twilight gloom
The pale crocuses lie gulping for air,
Gold among the tenacious green.

Pey Colborne

THE SWIFTNESS OF TIME

What happened?
Where did it go?
It went so fast!
But why, I do not know . . .

We all had so many plans,
So many ideas,
We wanted to share our thoughts
But we all believed; we had plenty of years . . .

But fate's plan . . .
Interrupted our love
To rip you from our grasp,
To take you to the Heavens above . . .

The tears that were shed,
Could have filled the sea,
And to this day we continue to weep,
I feel this remorse could last an eternity . . .

It has only been a few months,
And we still expect to hear your voice,
To hear you crack one more joke . . .
But silence fills the room; not one noise . . .

How cruel that life must go on,
To continue without you,
It seems so unfair,
That this would happen; that we never knew . . .

It hit us like a dagger,
One which was aimed for the heart,
But the feeling of love, I know we'll never be apart.

As these words of woe; are spoken strong and true,
Raymond Patrick Summerfield
Your family shall *forever* love; and miss you!

Belinda Louise Summerfield

MY GARDEN

The rhythmic sighing of the breeze
Ruffles the lacy blossom trees.
Banded honeybees softly whirr,
Drowsy black cats gently purr.
Cumbrous sunflowers standing tall
Jasmine clings to a sturdy wall.
Gauzy butterflies dive and pass
Daisies dapple the springy grass.
Blackbirds twirl their fluid notes
Ladybirds flash their scarlet coats.
Honeysuckle pervades the air
Everything I love is there.
My humble garden offers me
A place of sweet tranquillity.

Vivien Exall

WHO AM I?

I often ask myself
Who am I?
What is my identity?
The fact is, I don't know.

People only think about
Skin-deep features
Fat, thin, pretty, ugly
But they don't matter.

If everyone was the same
You wouldn't be judged
On how you look
Or talk or act.

Nobody truly knows
Who they are.

Who are we?
Who are you?
Who am I?

Leanne Mitchell (15)

DARE!

The salt laden gale funnelled up the scree
Whipping whins, broom, feathered plumes of bamboo tree
Snapping cane, whipping briar and bramble
Up zigzag walk, scree and tangle
Screeching birds in circle tight
Playing a dare, a nature fight.

A great skua from Outer Hebride
Likened the cliff to that at Innisfree
Thro' the spume, attacked the scree
Reckoning wrong, as was he
The whipping whins, briars lashing free
Forgetting, cliffs are bare at Innisfree.

From Hengisbury Head a great black back gull soared by
Took an interest, he would deign to try
Plunged towards the spume topped sea
His six foot span swept up the scree
A whipping bamboo plume caused his calamity
Fled in disgrace, so ashamed was he.

A solan goose from Sullum Voe
Decided he would also have a go
To win would enhance his name
As a flier of great renown and fame
His downfall was page 3 of The Sun
Entangled his legs and reputation.

The updraught like a mill race flies
Dare you, dare you! to my surprise
A gannet grey, dove to the sea
Turned to glide up the scree
Wingtip snarled on a whipping briar
Buffetted, bedraggled, ashamed of endeavour.

A Quinn

PEACE

Rambling through the woods
on a balmy springtime day
a sudden flash of colour
reveals our friend the jay.

Away from the traffic noise
there is an air of calm.
A rabbit plays quite openly,
no one to do him harm.

Robin chirping merrily,
calling his mate along.
She replying, darting, flying,
such a pretty song.

If we could linger here
for just an hour or two
forget the world outside,
so much good it would do.

Jean Ruddick

SUMMER EXPLOSION

Summer exploded one July golden coloured morning
Just as the sun crept over the horizon and a new day was dawning
Trees holding wide their branches of welcome to the morn.
As summer in all its magnificence was born
A flower that was once dormant unfurled crimson petals to the sky
Receiving the glowing heat of that golden orb
As though saying, 'Here am I'
Life bursting forth coaxed from the shy bud by the sun's fingered rays
Full green leaves, sensuous, bowed in adoration and praise
Of summer in all its splendid glory
A symphony of colour, red, green and gold
Revealing creation's story.

Mary Spence

THE GARDEN SENSES

The sight of flowers in full bloom
The sound of the cuckoo, its familiar tune
The smell of the freshly mown grass
The taste of berries from the fruit patch.
The feel of water from the garden stream
This is the garden senses dream.

J Hinson

THE BAT

Now there is an animal you may have seen
when you in old castles or churches have been,
which passes the winter exactly like that
'tis quite a common creature; its name is a bat!

In fine summer weather bats always come out,
when moths in the evenings are flying about,
for the bats feed on moths, and they think them as good
as you would think dinner or puddings for food.

Perhaps when you hear of a bat having wings, you will
think, like a bird, it has feathers and sings,
but its body is covered with soft, downy hair
and it looks like a mouse flying up in the air.

A bat cannot sing and of course, it can't speak
but sometimes it utters a shrill little squeak;
very much like a mouse, and at times it will hiss
but it's very frightened before it does this.

It never lays eggs in a hole in a house,
it brings up its little ones much like a mouse,
but instead of preparing a soft cosy nest,
it teaches its young ones to hang up to rest!

Now, if you should catch one, be sure that you look
at the joint of its wing for its strange little hook
and remember the story today, you have heard
of a creature that's both like a mouse and a bird!

Moira Round

MY HAVEN

Life has been so cruel
Good luck passed me by
Sometimes I feel so down
All I want to do is cry.

At times I could not carry on
My husband's violence never-ending,
Though I'd done nothing wrong
And when my baby daughter suddenly passed away
Any blue sky in my life suddenly turned grey.

But I have found a haven
A way to feel so free
Working in my garden
Or sitting by my tree.

Now I've begun a new life
Although sadness never leaves me
I'm busy in my garden
Planting flowers and a peace tree.

Gardening is therapeutic, makes worries fade away
Now my garden's beautiful I sit out here each day.
I have even built a pond
Could watch the fish swim away.

My garden is my haven
It's where I come to rest
And sitting underneath my tree
Is a place that I like best.

Ann Marie Chapman

NOVEMBER

As the dead leaves flutter from the branches,
And the cold wind sighs them away,
The ravaged earth is in mourning,
On this cold November day.

As sapless twigs fade away and fall,
In the smoky blue mists of the day,
We walk ankle deep in red-gold leaves,
As fog gathers thick and grey.

But there is beauty still in November,
As on holly boughs the crimson berries blaze.
The beech tree, she too keeps her foliage,
As burning red sunsets end our days.

Angela Dolphin

NORTH SEA

Toes and feet
Surrounded by the misty water
Of the reckless yet familiar North Sea
Paintings and letters scattered before me
So vehement in my own imagined demise
I long for release
The passing years have not made it better
Yet they promised me
Eventually time will heal
And although the English coast is my sanctuary
Today it is not my friend
And I have no sense to recognise
As I hold my hands up in surrender
That I have the power to let this go
And though your madness
Was once made beautiful in my eyes
For now it will only oppress me
As the sole cause of my potential demise
And the fear decided in my head
Is yet unwritten by Mother Nature
And at the point of sinking, I'm shaken by the words
My destiny is in my own hands
For though the past does not forget
The future does not remember.

Rebecca

UNTITLED

Summer days in the garden
Grass is green
Flowers blooming
Ready to burst
Fish swimming in the pond
Frogs jumping up and down
Stepping on stones
Bees humming
Ready for honey.

Pauline Morrow

A GARDENER'S POEM

I've hurt my back
And got the sack
From pulling up the weeds,
That's smothering all my seeds.
Sitting there in my chair
Hoping you'll grow through,
Into your blooms of blue.
Sunshine or rain
And in no pain,
I'll clean the soil for you.
Then you'll see that you'll be free
Of all that's stopping you.

E V Bowles

SPRINGTIME

The reeds on the riverbank tremble in the breeze.
Fresh new leaves shimmer and wave on the trees.
Birds flying frantic with twigs in their beaks
Making a home for their young in one or two weeks.
The river comes alive with swan and with duck,
Soon they too will have families with a little bit of luck.
Rabbits in the evening munching on the new grass
Shame to say these spring evenings will very soon pass.
As night falls, the birds' evening song will hold sway,
They seem to be shouting, 'It's been another perfect day.'

R C Durrant

SUMMER DREAMS

The sky fills with an illuminous glow,
As the sun creeps through the clouds.
The golden rays stretch across the sky,
Lightening up the world below.

Flowers raise their sleepy heads,
Dancing in the gentle breeze,
Gardens fill with fragrant scents,
As colour takes over, the once muddy beds.

The harmonious buzzing of the busy bees;
Occupy the sky,
Butterflies fluttering in the air,
As buds blossom high in the trees.

The sun twinkling on the silvery stream,
Light dancing in the rippling water,
New life beginning all around us
Summer's more than it seems!

S Short

WINNING A WOMAN

I know that you've been hurt before
I know - I've seen the pain
I know that walls surround your heart
I know - mine was the same
I know that you are waiting
I know - I'm waiting too
I know that love can move you
I know what it can do
I know that love is fragile
I also know it's steel
I know that love can hold you
I know how you should feel
I know you've taken refuge
I know you've closed the door
I hope you can be tempted
To open it once more.

Paul B Shipley

NUMB

I go to work every morning, open the coffee pot, pour the milk,
as I watch the milk pour I begin to realise that I am numb inside,
is it because I have no soul or no meaning in life.
I get on with my work each day, the same thing day in, day out,
flicking through papers and having no thought or care in the world.
I'm sure I have feelings if I look hard enough
but maybe that's not why I am numb,
maybe it's because I am missing something,
something so deep that I will never be able to find out what it is.
Will that mean I will always long for something for the rest of my life
and die knowing that I had never been a whole person,
a person who could have been happy just knowing they were whole
and not looking for that missing piece of the puzzle.
Should I keep looking and longing for the missing piece
or should I wake up and realise that life
is not always full of happiness and joy
and that I will have days when I am down and feel out of place,
but I should always remember I was put on this Earth to breathe,
to feel, to hear and to see,
maybe we should be grateful for what we have
and not always long for something bigger and better
as you might just already have it.

Nicole Bushe

THE PARROT NATION

I wish I were a parrot for
they don't spend their time
wondering how to win the war
or how to tackle crime.

The parrot nation's happy
just being who they be
why oh why, why oh why
why oh why aren't we.

The parrot rules the roost
without recourse to law
(tho' some might need a boost
when dealing with macaw)

Parrots don't use shops
of themselves they trust
and they don't pay cops
to keep 'em safe from lust.

Eric McCrossan

A GARDEN

What is a garden really for?
Growing flowers by the score.
Daffs and roses, poppies too.
Colours, of a different hue.

Plants and shrubs; trees as well.
The list is just too long to tell.
The splendour, of a smooth green lawn.
The birds that sing, at early dawn.

A squirrel too; you might just see
That visits from a nearby tree.
If you should see a heron bird:
Just watch your fishpond, mark my word!

The water features splash around
While insects scurry on the ground.
Each creature, with its natural talents
Keeps the vital eco, well in balance.

I use my garden, just for fun.
To laze around in the welcome sun.
So many things there, I can do,
Have a party, or a barbecue.

The garden shed houses my tools.
To help me keep, the seasonal rules.
This gift from nature's bounty brings
A host of truly wondrous things.

Sights and sounds, the sweet perfume,
Buds that blossom, into bloom.
What is a garden really for?
All these things, and so much more.

J E Davies

BIRD SONG

How sweet and gentle is the sound of birds at morning break,
To hear their tunes and melodies, a serenade to wake,
With jumping tails and shaken wings, perched high up in the trees,
They fill their chests and sing with joy no sweeter songs then these.

And as you waken from your sleep, to chirp and whistle blow,
Their chorus fills the air with song and off to work they go.
Soaring through the open sky, across meadows, fields and parks,
And resting in our gardens, sparrows, finches, tits and larks.

To bring us joy on waking, they lift our spirits high,
Imagine life without those singing creatures of the sky?
That bring you love in bird song, a chorus line complete,
To hear them sing from dusk till dawn their song of joy, so sweet.

So next time that you waken and drift to sleep at night,
If troubles fill your mind, hear our feathered friends of flight.
For their song can bring you comfort, a healing from above,
And *bird song* costs you nothing for it's given out of love.

Steve Ray Knight

WAVES

Moon drenched, the beach, it softly calls
I wander upon its rock-strewn shores.
The water whispers from hidden depths
The secrets it's so staunchly kept.
But oh, what tales the sea could tell;
Tales of Heaven, tales of Hell.
Each wave in turn a story breaks
And others come to fill its place.
One of fisherman Jim Macbride
And brother Michael, both who died
Out on the sea - a storm did break
And storm and sea both lives did take.
The sea it claimed both their lives
And kept their bodies - a morbid prize.
Another wave, another tale, a story of a mother whale:
Of a whale who swam too close, to a tiny fishing boat,
Who caught her tail in their lines
And couldn't get it free in time.
Another wave breaks on the shore
And yet another, more and more.
And now a happy tale at last,
One that happened long since past:
Of lovers walking hand in hand
At night across the silken sand.
Two lovers soon were man and wife
And walked the beach throughout their life.
The tales rekindle in the sand,
Then back to sea, then back to land.
I say to all, be still, sit tight
And listen to the waves at night.

Karen Louise Allen

NATURE'S TWIST

Friday was always - clock off
two pints, stiff double.
Home to relaxing weekend.

      The garden was clear.

Friday was clock off
two pints, stiff double. But . . .
slow reactions quick child.

      I planted a you tree.

Suspended sentence - heavy fine.
No recriminations from friends.
'Boy never looked - his fault.'

      It took root - began to bud.

Although normality surrounds
I can't seem to touch.
Life's becoming blanched

      The saplings in full bloom.

Cold eyes are watching.
Empty eyes are haunting.
'Is nobody listening.'

      Autumn leaves begin to fall.

Blood turns cold disembodied
while the moon smiles at his
reflection on the blade.

      Now the you tree is bare.

Maria Stewart

SPRINGTIME

Petals like confetti
Strewn across the ground
Reminding us that springtime
Once more, has come around

For all of those who notice
The red and pink and white
When daffodils have done their best,
Appears, another glorious sight.

The primroses have faded
Now grass is growing high,
Baby birds need feeding,
Dawn chorus hits the sky.

So the earth awakens
As sunbeams shower down
Warming soil, awaking seeds
Waiting to be grown.

Violets in the hedgerows
Shyly peeping thro'
Send forth perfume delicate
Gentle fragrance, true.

And so thro' all the length of days
With sun, some wind and rain,
The hedgerows and the gardens
Will come to life again.

Mariè Brown

My Garden

I look out of my window into my garden
and see my beautiful trees
and pink blossom in bloom,
the red rowan with berries so red,
the grass so green and lupins so blue,
and the roses in bloom,
and I thank God for all those things.

Chris McLeod

GARDENING

It's that time again, go to the shed,
Do the jobs people dread,
Mow the lawn, plant those seeds,
Sort out those weeds!
Sort out those tools, make the hedge thinner,
Clip it with a hedge-trimmer.
Just when you think that's the lot,
You remember those plant pots.
Finally with the jobs done,
Time to have some fun.
Deck chairs out, you know what to do,
Show your garden off with a barbecue!

Gwynfa Evans

IN THE GARDEN

In the garden I sit under the apple tree,
Listening to the birds and watching the bumblebee.
An assortment of seed ready to sow,
Growing green beans, row after row.
Each path edged with lavender sweet,
Window boxes full of pansies so neat.
Work to keep me busy for hours,
Digging, raking and picking flowers.
Pretty roses growing around the front door,
Pick potatoes, tomatoes, peas and much more.
Sitting on the bench, it's lovely and sunny,
A wooden beehive full of honey.
A greenhouse with sticks, trays, pots all mine,
Hoping every day the weather keeps fine.
Not a patch of the garden would be bare,
There's no place I'd rather be than there.
Watch little birds making their nests,
Lots of creepy crawlies and other pests.
Fragrant flowers, red, yellow, pink and blue,
Working, relaxing, there's lots to do.
Take my time at leisure,
The hours I spend there, it's a pleasure.

K Brown

IN THE GARDEN

Outside in the garden, what do you see? Lots of nice flowers
with a bench under the tree, then came all the birds, some magpies
black and white, others would be so colourful and bright, then change
colour in the light. Outside you would walk around to discover all the
things in the garden.

Claire O'Sullivan

THE CUCKOO

The cuckoo is so cunning and sly,
She lays in other nests, that's why!
The egg hatches and throws out the rest,
Everso cunning, I do not jest,
The donor bird works hard to feed
And pamper to its every need.
So whenever you hear the cuckoo calling
Think of the less fortunate ones, who were falling.

J H Christie

A VIOLET

Down in a green and shady bed
A modest violet grew.
Its stalk was bent, as if to hide from view,
Yet it was a lovely flower
Its colour, bright and rare
It might have graced a rosary bower
Instead of hiding there.

Patricia Treherne

APHRODITE'S LEGACY
(The Narcissi)

I begin to awake in darkness.
Trapped inside a mass of scale,
So I push upward till I am free
Of damp soil, then human hands
Gently sit me in light.

Now I catch my reflection
After dusk in a mirrored window.
I watch, as my stem grows taller -
Stronger and the weight of my beauty
Tilts my head to its best advantage.

Below me, the feeble crocus.
No confidence to show her face
Without the sun's encouragement.
Needing fancy pots to enhance her.
Above stands the gawky amaryllis
Her unkempt leaves and thick-set stem
Do little to help exhibit her
So again - I turn back to myself.

Enamoured by the beauty of my petals
Forming a star to surround my corona.
Inside which - my stamen are stiff
Their helmets covered in sweet pollen.

I am beautiful - I am beautiful

As she embalmed my spirit did Aphrodite
Know how exquisite this pain.
I keep watch till my freshness dims
Then slowly retreat into darkness.

Maria Germaine

STAND BACK AND ADMIRE!

With a cheerful smile on his face, he drove inside the driveway,
It has been a few years since he visited his good friend, TR.
As he glanced to his left, he couldn't believe his eyes!
He braked abruptly and stared wide-eyed, whistling softly,
He hopped out from his car and continued staring with disbelief.
Scratching the back of his head, he asked himself;
Is this the barren piece of land my good friend, TR.
Bought with the house some years ago?

Goodness me! I must stand back and admire!
Who would have thought all those half-dead plants he bought
From the marketplace
Would grow to such lushness!
He whistled loudly; What a transformation!
Look at all those variety of healthy glorious blooms!
Shining so radiantly in this, this sunny, spring afternoon!
'Hey? Hold on!' He suddenly said, deep in thought.

Just a moment! Tut! Tut! Goodness me!
I've made a terrible mistake! I'm in the wrong address!
'Uh-oh!' he chuckled cheerily; 'Am I going crazy or what?
I *am* at the right address! Blow me down!'
Heh! Heh! It's the transformation of this once barren land.
That had me puzzled! Just look at all those radiant blooms!
Well done, TR! Know what? I'll remain here a bit longer,
Just to stand back and admire!

Elsa Beggs

HOW NOW BROWN COW

The day I remember most
Is the day the rain washed all the cows brown.
I witnessed this from my car
As I drove along the motorway.
I had gazed upon the cows
On either side of the slab
For years I had driven up and down.

As a child, from my father's car windows
The window open; Yes I remember *now*.
The wind would fill my ears.
Down the country lane to Southport
I would see the cows and shout
'There's a cow, there's a cow and there's a cow.'

Recoiled memories now as then,
Would return out of the clear sunlight.
Since I could remember, the cows seemed
Like the plastic animals I would get for Christmas
In the plastic farm set, plastic sheep, dogs, people
The plastic tractor would lift plastic bales of hay
To the cows who were always black and white.

From these memories, my brain noticed something strange
Slowly on either side, in the green fields as the rain came down.
I put my wipers in full motion
They beat the rain as it drove into the windscreen.
I wiped the condensation from my side window
It seemed the rain had washed all the cows brown.

John A Duffy

FREE

Whether you are rich or you are poor
It's a great leveller being outdoors
When you look into the sky
And see nothing you can buy
Birds are there for you to see
'Yes', they are absolutely free
So are the country lanes to walk along
Take time to listen to a free birdsong
The lovely smell of fresh cut hay
And no one there to make you pay
Give the whole family a free day out
And something worthwhile to talk about
Find a tree to climb and a hill to roll down
And you'll be as happy as a circus clown
When you tell your friends at the end of the day
Of the fun you've had, with nothing to pay
I bet they don't tell you what they have done
Like queuing in a theme park that wasn't much fun

Stan Darby

MOTHER NATURE'S COUNTRYSIDE

Hills of high, valleys low,
the countryside we talk,
But have you considered going there
and taking a surprising walk.
Be it a local nature reserve,
or hills as far as they eye can see.
Mother Nature has some wondrous sights
awaiting you and me.
With rivers and streams weaving away
cutting through the land.
If you're lucky birds and wildlife of all sorts
could come, feeding from your hand,
Trees and flowers will wave at you
in the fresh country, breezy air,
To show you the kind of life they lead
and the wildlife that they share.
When you think you've finished looking
and what goes on all around -
Don't forget there's another world
down below the ground.

Peter Bayliss

LOCKED IN A CLASSROOM ON A SUMMER'S DAY

To be in history on a beautiful summer's day,
Does drive all joy and happiness away.
For when I try to focus on Peter the Great,
I find I cannot concentrate.
I gaze longingly through the windowpane,
To waste such a glorious day is such a shame!
My teacher does ignore my desperate cry,
And each minute of the hour does slowly drag by.
The radiance of the glowing sunlight does call to me,
How I long to be close to Mother Nature, wild and free.
Instead, I'm a caged bird.
Just another face among the herd.
In my books, I cannot find delight,
While the sun does shine so radiantly bright.
My heart fills with joy to hear the little sparrow sing,
A euphoric delight that no amount of teaching can bring!
How I wish that this lesson would simply end,
So I can rush outside and my restricted soul can rejuvenate and mend.
I sit in my seat and wish each second away,
Let us all go outside, dance, sing and play.
Take pleasure in what God has given us,
And be free and joyful as heavenly doves.
Let us all go outside and there we shall stay,
For nature was made to be worshipped
And praised all day.
But for goodness sake, let this torture end!
So my empty soul can release, revitalise and mend!

Summer Lili

SEASONAL WONDERS

On a bright April morn, I wake to birdsong,
At last it's spring, the winter so long.
Open the windows, see the sunshine,
Weather forecast, dry, warm and fine.
Looking out at skies of blue,
It so highlights, there's work to do.
I'm soon outside, breathing fresh air,
But my poor old garden's in need of some care.
So I get busy, first the lawn to mow,
Then find some seeds, I need to sow.
Next comes my fork, my rake and hoe,
A lot of work, we'll get a show.
I dig and dig and weed and weed,
I sow and plant and daily feed.
Day by day, they slowly grow,
In lines I've numbered, row by row.
Soon it's summer, my garden's in bloom.
Winter days forgotten of doom and gloom.
Colours galore, I glow with pride,
When all come and visit from far and wide.
But oh too soon, the nights draw in,
My blooms die off and grass grows thin,
Changing colours and leaves that fall
When autumn comes, why friends don't call.
To see my garden, nice chats and lingers,
And comments on why I was born with green fingers!

Sue Hetherington

NO IT IN AUTUMN

I stare at the roses
The red, white and pink
Then I wait for a while
And let myself think
Winter has gone
It's summer now
Summer, winter, autumn, spring
I hate all these weathers
When will I win?
Why can't they all stay the same
And stop being such a pain.
I hate the summer
When you get so hot
Hold on a second, I hate the lot.
Winter when you get so cold
Spring when all the flowers
Are new, not old
And autumn, oh yes, I hate autumn
Because it doesn't rhyme with *IT*.

Lily Carmen Pepper

LITTLE LEAF

This little leaf, I hold in my hand,
Not too much bigger than a few grains of sand.
It's scarlet, velvet, bruised,
However now its life is used.

All of its life, it must have seen
Animals that have come, gone and been.
Hedgehogs, rolled into a ball
From its viewpoint, high and tall.

On misty days with faded grass,
People would walk up the dusty mountain pass.
Or is there something it has missed?
A glimpse of phantoms in the mist.

On days of sun, laughter and fun,
All the people would flock and come
To see view of towns afar.
A camper sat with a guitar
Or is there someone in the trees?
Hidden among the thicket of leaves.

The poor beautiful leaf,
Is now in a Christmas wreath.
It never stood a chance from its branch,
It was tore
Now it's on somebody's door.

Daniel Ambrose (13)

NATURE SMILES

From a little blade of grass to a tree that stands up tall
Through winter and through spring, through summer
And through fall, Nature smiles.
Daffodils and bluebells, roses, big and small
Snowdrops in the garden, flowers to suit us all.
A hedgerow, thick with foxglove, a yellow field of maze
The sweetest smell of honeysuckle all dance on summer days
Tiny little shoots that spring up from the ground
In all these flowers everywhere, there's beauty to be found
In your garden standing tall or your window, small and neat
It doesn't matter where or how, for us they're such a treat
The seeds of all those flowers travel for miles and miles
They grow for us, so we can see, just how Nature smiles.

Margaret Taylor

ROAD RUNNER

The pheasant
Is
A pleasant
If
A slightly
Scatty bird.
Its voice
Is
Quite distinctive
And
Its plumage
Is
Superb.
Why is it
Then
When I am
Driving down
A
Country lane
This handsome
Batty bird
Thinks
Harry Kerry
Is
Its name?

A Mayne

THE WITCHES' WISHING WELL

On Sabbath, at the witchen dell,
At owl-light among the mice and bats;
With a wave of a wand, the shimmering fish pond
Is transformed into a wishing well.

Here, the coven meet and cackle,
Egged on by the high blood moon.
They collect toadstools, dance with tricky ghouls;
Eat frogs' legs by the sack full.

They stoke the flames beneath the cauldron,
Stir in beetle blood, eyes of newt.
Round the bubbling broth, they darn their black cape cloth
And drink large goblets of strong blue ruin.

Sopped with gin, they wave their wands,
Turn foe to worms or spiders' webs;
Add the candle snuff to the fiery froth,
Incant their wishes, one by one.

'Zing! I wish for red elf-locks.'
'Bazoo! Grant me a wicked charm.'
'Doodle dim! To woo my sooterkin,
Please furnish me with fishnet socks!'

Moon's women plying their trade at night,
They plough the fertile soil of March;
Under the astral sign of fire, sow their sweet peas 'midst the briars,
While a charm to Diana, they recite.

Night leaves the sky in swirls of dusky rose,
Daybreak rouses the witches from sleep.
And with a *tap, tap, tap* from their big black cat,
They turn back into a flock of nesting crows.

Carly Dugmore

THE NEVER-ENDING SAGA

I bought myself a crossbow from a catalogue for kids;
It was only meant for targets but I modified it. I did,
And now a crop of arrows await the first outbreak
Of this year's crop of squirrels, no mercy will I take.
Painted bright red, so's they won't get lost,
As they hurtle near and far.
Makes the little devils jump
For this is truly *war!*
Thus it was that spring passed by
My aim, improving ever;
Now summer's here, I'm additionally cursed
By lumps of fluff and fevver!
Pigeons that is; descending in droves
To rob the small birds of their seed,
But as with the squirrels, my bowstring will twang
And cure the fat brutes of their greed.
Beasts are now becoming wary,
Flocks of arrows exceedingly scary.
A few weeks peace . . . there and then
Here the buggers come again!

Stan Kay-Walton

SPRING (PERESEPHONE)

Spring! She is the season in two parts
The growing seed - the purest heart.
The vital grain that ever feeds
The earth and all mankind now needs.

Alive and potent - yet so mild
She gently nurtures nature's child.
The corn, the wheat, the fruit and flowers
She endows with all her powers.

Yet soon she will just fade away
Deep underground her part to play.
She procreates with every breath
Goddess of generation and death.

M P Johnson

WHEN SUMMER COMES

Flowers start to
Show their heads
As summer spreads,
Far and wide
Things start
To come alive
Fresh leaves showing
On the trees,
Birds singing
Their best songs
Hoping to attract
A new mate before long,
Baby lambs jumping
To and fro
Not worrying which
Way they go,
Bees rushing
Here and there
Carrying as much
Pollen as they dare
Too much
They might drop and die
Before reaching
The hive alive,
These are some
Of the things
Summer brings.

Frank Thomas

SECRETS OF THE SEA

I placed a shell next to my ear,
I close my eyes, what can I hear?
I hear the whispers of the sea,
I hear the waves, they're calling me:
Rushing forward, then rushing back,
This great wall of water, so scary and black.

My head is full of distant echoes,
Which fill the corners of my mind.
Wild white horses rushing inward,
Exposing hidden shells, I'll later find,
Sand gently churning, seaweed twirling;
These murky depths have untold tales.

With my ears I can hear -
With my mind I can imagine,
As the secrets of the sea unfolds.

Rita Algar

SPRING TIME

The best time of the year is definitely spring,
All the trees blossom and the birds all start to sing.
The sun begins to shine again and makes the world glow,
And in every park the flowers start to grow.

The nights start getting longer so there's more time to play,
Lambs, chicks and bunny rabbits are born every day.
All the baby animals grow and start to use their legs,
And all the children stuff their faces with Easter eggs.

Bees all start to buzz again and butterflies appear,
Everybody's happy because holidays are getting near.
Spring has now ended and now summer's come around again,
It will be back soon but there's plenty to look forward to
Until then!

Amanda Baldwin (14)

LABOUR OF LOVE

You tenderly put me in rich, moist soil.
You kept me warm and watered.
It was dark but I felt safe,
One day I saw the light and felt the warmth on my frail limbs.
You spoke to me and showed me to your friends.
Every day I grew stronger, you were always there for me.
Then one day, I remember well, you were so excited.
I had started to repay back your kindness and hard work.
My flowers turned to fruits and I could see how proud you were of me.
Your day soon came to reap your rewards,
My strawberries were picked and made centre-piece on the table for tea.

Karen M Green

ENJOY YOUR WEEDS

Garden weeds aren't just a scourge -
they may be beneficial -
help to nourish cultivars,
like dandelion and thistle

Ground ivy - 'gill creep by the ground'
- sow thistle or 'milky dickle'
like to spread themselves around
have rather pleasant tickle!

Chickweed makes an eye lotion;
yarrow helps to treat a cold;
dandelions are good for gout,
inflammation of the toes

Clover's good for whooping cough;
silverweed protects your skin;
had a touch too much of sun?
- let healing power of weeds begin!

Stinging nettles loves to settle
in your nettle bed for free -
it's a plant of hardy fettle -
great for making nettle tea!

Kenneth Berry

THE SENSORY GARDEN

Tall sunflowers basking in the autumn sun
A boat shaped flower bed with a seat, makes it fun
A squirrel runs along the grey stone wall
Blue tits all twittering their merry call
A song thrush we see, it gives us a thrill
Trees loaded with berries, he eats his fill
Different coloured tiles, side by side
Placed by students with glowing pride
The terracotta pots with their dying flowers
Having given their best in the summer hours
Three stone faces staring into space
Contemplating this garden place
The summer house with its welcoming seat
Ponder awhile in this pleasant retreat
Tall grasses bending with a gentle sway
Among the flowers, a colourful display
Orange marigolds and cornflowers blue
The seedpods with their autumn hue
So take your drinks and stay awhile
The Sensory garden will make you smile

B M Beatson

In the Country

Going to the country for a day out,
Seeing what nature is all about,
Along narrow lanes, I go by car,
Knowing the journey will not be far.

Mountains and fields with meadows too,
There's plenty in the country for me to do.
Walks with picnics, the animals as well,
All around me the hills and the fell.

I see cows grazing in the grass,
And from field to field slowly they pass.
Little lambs that jump up so high,
With not a care as the world hurries by.

Horses lying down, side by side,
Gazing around with eyes open wide.
Lakes with water that lies so still
And ducks that float at their own will.

Streams from which waters do gush,
Rabbits running from bush to bush,
Woods with trees where squirrels play,
Hiding their nuts from day to day.

All kinds of creatures you will see,
If you take a ride along with me,
A day in the country you won't forget,
And one I know you won't regret.

Lilian Florence Jones

UNTITLED

Dew cries over shoulder blades
As morning breathes down the necks of trees
Seeds parachute from flower faces
Avoiding stone with soft earth dreams
The worm boldly periscopes for feathered foe
Before blindly approaching the day in dark
On closer inspection, the line of ants
Make pieces of leaf, their earthly sails
Bouncing bomb bees break for nature dams
As leaves line up for free-fall fun
Web repairs take place upon a silent breeze
As last night's prizes twitch to still
The four winged fury of the flying dragons
Are mirrored above rivers of glistening gold
Black cab beetles catch the sunlight's glint
As they scuttle for first in a rockery race
The scent of summer mixed in airstreams
Means boiling point melts tarmac skin
The coming 'ready or not' sky seeks hidden clouds
As green dehydrates into a longing for rain
Sun releases its grip on the afternoon's throat
And let's evening splutter in on a crest cool wave
Temperature takes the weight off its heat
Leaving activity to jigsaw in the playground of birds
The lowered pinks of a proverb sky
Mean it will soon be punched black and blue by stars
Before the silver circle signal welcomes the night's guests
Leaving only sonar noise to fill the empty remains
Hollow and patient life blinks before rebirth
At the suspecting world of overlooked joys.

Marq Sutton

MY GARDEN

Sitting here in my deckchair,
In the garden, the weather's fair.
Winter's over, spring's begun,
Time to clear, the garden done.
Hedges now tidy, grass so long,
Listen to the birds, in full song.
Motivation is what I need,
To cut the bushes and tend the weeds.

I've trimmed the hedges, cut the lawn,
Worked from sunset until dawn.
On my knees, the weeds I fight,
Pulling hard, with all my might.
Bulbs I planted in the fall,
Showing through the Earth, some are very tall.
Flowers will soon appear
Because it is the time of year.

Now I have the pond to clean,
Soon the fish will be seen,
As they surface to the top.
Watch the frogs on the lilypad's hop.
Children safely in the garden play,
Enjoying the sunshine, long may it stay.
Birds in the bird bath, drink and bathe,
Away from the cats, in the bushes lay.
Insects, underneath the stones,
Bees busy taking the pollen home.
Butterflies with beautiful colour; sit on the nettles,
Their silk, delicate wings, look like petals.

Evening comes, sun goes down,
Then the night life call around,
Hedgehogs, scurry to and fro,
Sly old fox watches where they go.
Now it's time for me, to go to bed,
Thoughts of gardening, out of my head.
Looking forward to a new day
In the garden, we can rest and play.

Marilyn Pullan

EAGLE OWL

The eagle owl winked at me,
talons clenched, head proud,
immaculate gown of mottled down
aquiline, still.
A torpid lid lifted,
omniscient outlook
poured toward me;
one-eyed glower of the owl's
portentous power;
far, far-seeing bird,
unflinching in somniferous
captivity,
sending the searing,
present-piercing stare
of the seer . . .
Seeing
without saying,
knowing
without going,
world without cages,
Amen.

Michael Kelly

SPRING

When the long winter nights have finally past
And the light of day begins to last
Mother Nature takes command
And orders spring to green the land

The meadow flowers burst into bloom
'Neath the merry trill of the skylark's tune
Trees begin to show their bud
Adding colour to the bare stark wood

The golden rape and the cornflower blue
Give the patchwork fields a colourful hue
In contrast to the ploughed-up fields
Which will provide the farmer, his vegetable yields

Creatures of the countryside
Begin their searching, far and wide
To find a mate and build a home
To raise a family of their own

In the household gardens people are busy
Planting petunia and busy lizzie
Whilst beetles and ants scurry and toil
Creating movement amongst the soil

The voracious ladybird spends the day
Munching aphid pests away
Leaving buds and stems all clean
For flowers to produce their petals of sheen

Mother Nature's yearly chore
Has blossomed and greened the land once more
So let us, to her, our praises sing
For this magical season that we call spring.

Harry Miller

SEASONS

The trees are green, the flowers bloom
The sweet fragrance fills the air
It's summer now but when winter comes
The trees will be stark and bare

Search little robin, search
Build your nest and thrive
When the snow covers the land
You will fight to stay alive

Little field mouse, small and brown
Have you stored your winter fare?
You've built your home with grass and down
You'll be snug and warm in there

Look the snow it's melting fast
The spring begins to come
Little animals you're alright now
Warmed by the summer sun.

The Earth is such a wondrous sight
The seasons come and go
The trees and plants come to life
As their leaves begin to grow.

Janet Mears

GOD'S NEW CITY

When this old world shall pass away
God's new city we should see;
If we have lived to serve Him well
Then with God we hope to be.

There shall be no more crying,
There shall be no more night.
No need for sun, moon or candle,
God's glory will be the light.

No more tears and no more sin,
No more pain or sorrow.
No more death or curse or sea,
There is no tomorrow.

May we in simple faith draw nigh
Lead us to the living fount above,
And never to another fountain fly;
Hold us loving God within Thy love.

We walk God's city of pure gold
The walls of precious stones,
Where God's angels lead us
Through gates that never close.

Oh to dwell in God's new city
With pure water oh so bright
Cascading from the throne of God and Lamb,
In the midst, the Tree of Life.

Oh the beauty, oh the wonder,
Of God's new world up above,
To dwell with Him in Heaven
In the glory of His love.

Vi Berriff

A Midsummer Night's Dream

I know a place where the sun glows,
Where trees, grass and flower grows,
Pixies dance among the bees,
With dwarves eating by the trees.

Fairies fly in their dreams,
With pixies swimming in the streams,
Dwarves are in the forest deep,
And the sun is rising while they sleep.

I know a place where the river flows,
Where sleeping fairies and daises doze,
The roses awake by the sun's gleam,
Of a midsummer night's dream.

Bethany Jones (13)

ALL SEASONS

When one writes poems or love songs they nearly always
write about spring
Of the birds, the green grass and flowers and the wonderful
colours they bring.
Take winter, with its glistening frost and what looks nicer
than a snow clad tree?
Then of course we have the lambs and the chicks that come with spring.
With the birds feeding their young and flying from tree to tree
as they whistle and sing.
Around the corner is summertime
With those lovely hot days, when the sun throws its rays
and we lounge about, feeling relaxed and sublime.
Followed by autumn with the nip in the air
as you walk in the country with the winds in your hair.
Walking through scattered leaves of brown and gold
If you wrap up warm, you don't feel the cold.
Why sit at home, like bees in a hive
When you can prepare yourself, whatever the weather
and feel glad to be alive.

I Lee

THE GARDEN

The grass grows tall
The sun is hot,
The flowers do bloom
A lot.
The bugs and bees do buzz
The birds do sing.
The trees have fruit
The wasps do sting.
Summer is here not
The spring.

J T Hazell

A SUNNY DAY IN 1932

It was a lovely summer's day
We walked to Lymes Park, so far away
We watched the graceful deer drinking from the lake,
Relaxed beneath an oak tree and ate a cherry cake.
I make a yard-long daisy chain
Soon to wither - what a shame!
A dandelion seed settled on my frock
'Tell me is it two o'clock?'
We climbed the hill where wild berries grew
And ate them 'til our lips turned blue.
We watched a Red Admiral butterfly
Land on a beautiful rose nearby.
My thoughts returned to days of yore
When leaves turn to gold, I'll return once more.
Oak and ash - I'll press quite a few,
To remember the summer in 1932.

Edna Kitchen

CARE OF OUR COUNTRYSIDE

This wonderful earth was a gift from above.
Let us therefore protect it with kindness and love.
So in the future: generations to come,
Will be able to say, 'They thought of us some.'

Let us leave to them, the birds and the bees,
The rivers, the mountains, flowers and trees.
So that when they breathe, we must ensure,
That the air that they breathe is 100% pure.

The woods have gone, one no longer sees
The open glades and towering trees.
The Ragwort, Vetch and Wiry Fern,
Have all diminished to the farmer's 'burn'.

From the fields and woods, the rabbits have gone,
And the trout in the stream, well we have none.
No more do we hear the Corn Crake's call,
No more do we see the elm leaves fall.

The kingfisher now, is almost extinct,
The curlew too, is on the brink.
The trees are stripped, down my old lane,
Thanks to the scourge of acid rain.

The cliffs and the shores to the tern are a haven,
The crags and the rocks are home to the raven.
The valley and woods where the kite has its nest,
Must never be marred by man's greed and zest.

What once was protected from damage and harm,
Has now all gone under the intensive farm.
In my generation, our loss is so vast,
If it goes on like this, we just cannot last.

So please protect our countryside,
And try to save it far and wide,
And make a pledge and final solution,
To rid this earth of filth and pollution.

J Jones

IN MY GARDEN

In my garden there would be
Hollyhocks, roses and an old apple tree.
A luscious lawn, I need to keep mowing
Every week of course, for the grass keeps growing.
I'd have a pond with a garden gnome,
Here at my cottage. I'd feel at home.
In my garden the children would play.
Saying 'Hello Nan, we've come to stay!'
Window boxes and patio tubs,
Lavender bushes also plenty of shrubs.
In my garden. I'd sit out all day
From early morning till the sun went away.
I'd have barbecues in the warm evening air.
A few friends over, a drink we would share.
Over the fence with neighbours I'd chat,
But this is all a dream, as I live in a flat!

Lynne Clements

IT HAD TO GO

'It's your birthday soon,' I said to the wife.
'A very special time of life.
Is there anywhere you would like to go
To celebrate the big five-O?'
'I don't think so,' she said with a grin,
Finger tapping against her chin.

'I would like a greenhouse to sow some seeds,
It's just the thing my garden needs.'
'There's no room!' I blurted out
'Oh yes,' she said, 'there is no doubt,
Your brick-built barbie will have to go,
It's no use to us in rain and snow.'

So down it came, brick by brick,
Strewth and blimey, was I sick.
No more half-cooked burgers and Aussie lager
Now it's jasmine and saxifraga
As tomatoes flourish and seedlings grow
My brick-built barbie just had to go!

John Simpson

DUTY BOUND

The prize was bright, so pretty to see,
The fair-haired youngster looked straight at me.
The prize you see, was out of bounds
Among other things, it was on private grounds.

I stood with spade; a well earned breather
And watched the face of this little creature.
Eyes fixed with wonder and determined face -
Fingers on lips, eyes shaded by lace.
She - herself, being of beauty and grace.

The elderly hands, arms, a little relaxed,
Given moments of freedom to this precious catch.
A skip, a jump, unsteady walk,
The joy too much to waste - reaching hands to take the prize
She pulled with frown and haste
The prize, so reluctant to be plucked,
Held her ground with grace.
Dirt on face and eyes a-shine,
Her little hand reached out for mine.

The little face turned again to me
Eyes begging for the prize to be.
I bent down and plucked this wanted beauty
And presented this prize - I felt it my duty.

The joy was not only hers you see,
That man that planted that flower, was me.

G J Hancock

SERENITY

The sun beats down, my mouth is dry
The air is filled with wasp and fly
If I just had a magic wand
To wave at hedge and grass and pond
A calmer life would be for me
Not that of a demented flea
The grass it grows a foot a day
Just can't keep the slugs away
Cats have dug up all my seeds
And I lost the tortoise in the weeds
Scratched myself on a thorny rose
My feet got tangled in the hose
I have to forge ahead today
The weatherman says rain on the way
But maybe I should have a rest
I know I did my very best
Still looks as bad as when I started
Now I really am disheartened
A cup of tea is what I seek
I'll leave it for another week.

P Cannon

THE SUNFLOWER

I stand alone so proud so tall
And watch my friends as raindrops fall
They hang their heads as if in shame
But have no choice of who to blame
And then the sun appears in view
And all the flowers awake on cue
They turn their heads as if to say
We've come alive to meet the day
We wait a while and friends appear
To whisper stories without fear
So many flowers, soft but bold
Share my life but I've grown old
So who will take my place just now
And keep my friends from harm, but how.

Dorothy Haywood

FLOWER

Bare you are
Just a stem
Waiting to flourish
Into life

A drip, a drop
You start to grow,
Grow and grow.

Your beautiful petals
Open wide until
You become a beauty of colour
So you hold on to
Light, air and water
To stay alive and fuller.

Lauren Angela Curley

THE GARDEN

Oh little rose how sweet you are,
Your perfume lingers from afar,
As paradise unfolds
Your worth more than gold.

A little gnome in the corner,
Watching over the flower border,
Next to the grass verge
A blue pot of herbs.

Trees stand tall
Petals softly fall,
Birds on the wing
As they whistle and sing.

A carpet of colour,
As I sit and wonder,
Delight with all reasons
A garden for all seasons.

Frances Rankine

FLOWERS

Flowers

To walk among the flowers
To smell their perfumed heads
To see the wondrous colours
As they grow among the beds

The Wren

The wren is singing sweetly
On the conifer above,
He sings, to tell his sweetheart
'Our nest is ready now my love.'

M Perkins

SEASONS FOUR

The winter snow is melting fast
The cold days fading out
The year begins to pass us by
Soon spring will be about
And then alive will come the trees
The flowers and the honey bees
Birds will sing and fill the sky
Newborn lambs, a welcome cry
Children playing, having fun
Along then comes the summer sun
People dashing here and there
Packing cases everywhere
Eager to be on their way
To foreign lands, far away
And when the running seems to stop
Autumn leaves begin to drop
Pretty colours, golds and browns
Falling lightly to the ground
Migrating birds ready to fly
Gathering in the autumn sky
And then it's quiet and not a sound
The rabbits all gone underground
Above so overcast and grey
The winter months, well on their way
Then it's Christmas, bells will ring
Carols, all the people sing
And then it's over, we are left no doubt
A new year in, the old one out
And so revolving round once more
We'll start again, all seasons four.

Arthur T Blakemore

SPRING

Today I went for a gentle walk
Being along there was no need to talk
You can look around and admire the view
All for free and it is all new
How many times do we walk not seeing a thing?
Wrapped up in our thoughts of what life is to bring
But, if you stop for just one minute
Gaze at the beauty
You will see what is in it
The flowers and the trees
The blossom and the smell
It is so beautiful, how are we to tell
Or explain, what Mother Nature gives us to see
And appreciate each day
What we all get and is for free.

A Roach

VICTORIA'S WALLS

A grey granite island,
an atoll of gangland atonement.
Its citizens hide in a society of shadows,
here doors slam shut on the just and deserted,
keeping out all but the clean air of freedom,
which kisses each convict a promise,
that their hell is not harboured alone.

I walk the longing corridor of the dead,
where the common were brought to book and prayer,
where lasting innocence ditched its tears
- in letters of ending love.
They clung to stolen straws of psalm,
in sure and certain hope,
yet revelation came at eight, remanded in a rope.

Now only stony secrets remain,
Her Majesty's mortar repents to the touch,
the bricks rebound with embattled lament,
Pierrepoint's play performs no more,
compassion has masked and strangled the scaffold,
absolving the dogs who died in its war.

Still one young pup snarls from the landing
- liberty's last suitor.
The world outside is a pearl beyond price
- a gem held just out of reach.
His defiance gleams in a life of grime,
his defence is a date with a different hangman,
the day of the open door,
when bars must melt, for their collars are felt
and locks all fall to the floor.

Sean Kinsella

A WINTER GARDEN

As dawn is breaking into day,
What a glittering display.
Grass with snow is lightly dusted,
Spider's webs all jewel encrusted.
Trees and shrubs a pattern trace,
As intricate as hand-made lace.
Washing lines that catch the light,
Each bedecked in diamonds bright.
Icicles all sharp and clear,
Like a crystal chandelier.
Where border had in water lain,
Now mirrored pools of frozen rain.
The spruce, a tall and stately sight,
Dressed in tinsel, glistening white.
But as the sun awakes, I fear,
This wonderland will disappear.
Though Mother Nature leaves behind,
A lasting image in your mind.

Trish Lomas

THE SQUIRREL

As I walked by the roadside,
One fine summer's day,
A sweet little creature
Headed my way:
She was a red squirrel,
As cute as can be,
And she suddenly darted
Past the stump of a tree!
Her coat was so glossy,
Her eyes were so true,
And I loved her so dearly;
This instant I knew!
With a tail like a bushel,
And fur soft as fleece,
I hope that her journey
Such joy will release.

Sharon Howells

THE HEDGEHOG'S LAMENT

It was not a dignified end
Not the end he would have wished for
Not a quiet passing away in a warm bed of leaves
Surrounded by family
Or in the dark, dank burrow that was his earthly home

No, a thousand sharp quills
Was no match for the Pirelli print
That bore down and passed so swiftly on
In the quiet country lane that was his habitat
A phrase 'the quick and the dead' springs to mind

At least it was quick

Patricia Jennings

THE SOUNDS OF SPRING

See the birds, hear them sing, as they all welcome in the spring,
Hear the bees buzzing to and fro, watch the flowers swiftly grow.
Hear the water falling into the pond, gentle droplets forming a bond.
Hear the distant croak of the frog, there he is sitting on that log.
Feel the warmth of the spring sun, at last we know winter is done.
All we need now as the days pass by, is to see the swallows
$\qquad\qquad\qquad\qquad\qquad\qquad$ high in the sky.
And we listen to the first cuckoo song, in May would be best
$\qquad\qquad\qquad\qquad\qquad\qquad$ to keep our summertime long.
But you know all seasons have their own magical wonder that
$\qquad\qquad\qquad\qquad\qquad\qquad$ makes us stop, listen and ponder.
But no matter what magic they bring, my favourite season
$\qquad\qquad\qquad\qquad\qquad\qquad$ is the season of spring.

M Hooton

A FOXY TALE

With bushy tail, brown eyes unwinking
The young brown fox is quietly slinking
Avoiding hounds that are pursuing
With men on horses loudly hooting

The hounds again now have his scent
And he must run in dire torment
The river's close he senses now
He must escape this pack somehow

To swim across was his intention
But local floods now in contention
With baying hounds now in full voice
To stay alive he has no choice

He plunges in and tries to swim
The river closes over him
A bough that's broken in the wind
Comes to his aid to which he clings

The river into which he sank
Sweeps bough across to furthest bank
He has survived a tale to tell
When he gets home to Dingley Dell.

Ronald H Blee

LADYBIRD

Ladybird, oh ladybird do fly away,
You see this is a nice summer's day.
Your lovely red coat and big black spots,
With lots of tiny little dots.
You are a delicate insect and so very small,
Thank you for coming to visit me by landing on my wall.
You crawl along my hand and feel so light on my skin,
Then you fly away for another friendship to begin.

Louise Mortimer (16)

THE WILLOW COTTAGE

Flowers are blooming bright and so clear
Bulbs are appearing so heavenly near
Snowdrops like flakes of snow which come then go
Blankets of flowers from path to path
So heavenly beneath the grass
Butterflies fly to and fro, like fairies they up and go
Winds are gentle, blowing autumn will soon appear
Yes the time is also near, I shed a tear
The flowers no more to be, they gently go beneath the snow
Waiting, waiting for me.

Nina

My Garden

There are treasures in my garden
Come, share them now with me
Perhaps a lovely butterfly
Or a busy bumblebee
Worms that burrow underground
Put air into the soil
And birds of many species
Begin their daily toil
I lift a piece of rotting wood
And what do I behold?
A big black toad is hiding there
Sheltering from the cold
I gently put the wood back
It's his home, after all
Perhaps quite soon his mate will come
And he waits for her to call
A blackbird sits upon the roof
Just listen to his song
Oh! How it lifts my heart up
And I know where I belong
My garden was my pride and joy
But now I'm racked with pain
If I get down on hands and knees
I can't get up again!
Although my bones have softened
And my knees refuse to bend
I still enjoy my garden
For its pleasures never end.

Rhoda D Ribbens

SPARROWS POND

On the bright lake alone I sit
With lilies still in the quiet wind
On the bright lake alone I sit
Waiting for an estranged friend

The bulbous forests surround me
And the good green reeds bend
The bulbous forests surround me
But where is my estranged friend?

The moon clouds flicker now it's night
Under the bright spiral of stars
Winds scramble through busy groves of trees
And darkness has fallen on the paths

Daniel Miles

WHISPERING

See the little branches
Twist and turn toward you
Patiently they wait for buds
Outstretched toward the sky

They wave to you with love
They whisper to and fro
Fingers, arms and trunk have they
And roots down far below

Their roots are soaked with love
And reach down underground
The love it flows up through them
To fill the world with sound

Their leaves, their flowers and blossoms
Will very soon be here
Patiently they wait for you
A special time of year

And very soon they'll start again
A circle, this is true
And when the first of spring appears
We'll bring again anew.

April Dickinson-Owen

SEEDS FOR TOMORROW

What are you doing
that is taking
so much time out there?

Your back to the wall
your face to the earth
and bottom to the skies

What are you doing
that is taking
so much out of you,
when all you can do
is go out there
when I am inside,
watching you, as
you stare towards hell?

You're planting the seeds
for tomorrow, you say,
and they'll be up soon
(That will be the day!)
It's just as well
the pleasure is in planting,
for they'll blossom
a million miles away.

Linda Kettle

4 SEASONS

Four seasons of green foliage,
With colours and the flower,
With tools and green fingers,
The gardener's source of power.
Air, wind, sun and rain,
Aids fruit, veg, herbs and nuts,
The extra survival,
Inside glass, sheds or huts.
Trees, grass and woodland,
Seeds, bulbs and pots,
Countryside and gardens,
Plots, all in lots.
Stone, wood and soil,
Wildlife, hedge and weeds,
Learning to cope,
Against pests and disease.
Perennials, biennials,
Annual, year after year,
With a trowel and a fork,
The compost and shears.
Tropics, and cacti,
Topiary and rose,
Fence, gates and walls
Ornaments do pose.
The watery garden,
With ponds and a stream,
The glistening, trickle
That sounds fresh and clean
The beauty and perfume
Creating a dream.

Jane Abbott

THOR!

The mighty Thor is not dead yet
I heard him from my window
For where would we be if we could not get wet
Sweating, yes, sweat on a pillow.

He sang twice as though in debt,
For all that beast has furrowed
And now since the sun has set
He may sing out tomorrow.

I love you Thor, an eternal bet
That you will ease my sorrow
And as the earth dies we may photosynthesise
And repay all we borrow.

Cliff Holt

STOP, LOOK AND LISTEN

It's whispering in the wind
It's echoing through the glen
The tragedy of our wildlife
Just what's happening to them?

Oh why is the greed of man
Destroying everything that's good
Stealing the sound of our song thrush
Silencing the voice of the wood

Poisoning our fields with chemicals
Giving insects and birds not a glance
Why can't they stop, look and listen
And for once give nature a chance

What do you want to wake up to in the morning
To birdsong and nature's dream
Or a boring fence with red paint on
Where a choir and a hedgerow has been

For together we are helping to ruin
What God and nature has given us
The Barn Owl without a barn
The bee without a buzz

For we have lost half of our wildlife
In the last twenty years
If we carry on with this merciless slaughter
Wildlife itself will disappear

So when you get up in the morning
Plant a hedge instead of a fence
Then the next generation will thank you
For at last using some commonsense

Politicians must stop aggressive farming
Go back to years now gone
When chemicals were nothing but a pipe dream
And on our fields only manure was put on

For life is a vicious circle
And the bad and good will come round
So let's stop and listen to what nature's telling us
Stop this pollution of our sacred ground.

Doug Downton

SPRING

Winter is long, gloomy and cold,
With snow and ice, to go out you're bold.
But spring is coming, it won't be long,
We'll soon here the birds in full song.

The daffodils, crocus and flowers so bright,
The lovely fresh smell of blossom, the buds on the tree,
The lawn now growing, as lush as can be.

I can sit in my garden, with newspaper and tea

Yes spring is here, and it will do for me.

Dee Degnan

THIXENDALE

(With apology to Alfred, Lord Tennyson)

I come from Yorkshire, born and bred,
Some people call me Sally.
I live in 't 'Crack', or so it's said
By dwellers in this valley.

By sixteen vales one can come down
To climb among the ridges,
Or travel to the nearest town
Ten miles across the bridges.

A tiny village, Thixendale,
Lost in a valley bottom,
Combining neatly in the vale;
Once seen, but ne'er forgotten.

Sara Ward

MY FOUR-LEGGED FRIEND

He looked at me, as much as to say,
What are we doing in the garden today?
Not a lot! I heard myself pledge,
Just weed around and cut the hedge.
Mow the lawn - trim the edges too,
Water the plants - we'll soon be through.
I heard a sigh, and looked around,
His body was spread eagled on the ground.
With paws fixed firmly over his face,
The posture portrayed, he's not moving a pace.
I gave it a thought, and fully agreed, so
Pulled out a chair - with gathering speed.
And now all there is to say
The gardening can wait for another day.

H Griffiths

SEASONS

Seasons
they are a
changing
Chill has gone
from the earth.

Summer heralds
misty mornings
On the hill and
glen
New day is
dawning

From field afar
one little lamb
is born
This misty morn

Our world of
seasons
A bird song
cries

Wilhelm

DID YOU SEE THAT?

Oh not again, did you see that?
Look, pecking furiously, oblivious to us,
Here comes the ginger Tom from next-door,
Off flies fat robin after a whack off his paw.
She's late today, the kitchen door is closed,
I'm ready for my lunch,
I hope there'll be buttered breadcrumbs,
Nuts and my favourite biscuit crunch.
Did you see that? Greedy squirrel, lives in the other tree,
He's always looking for food
And he hates me.
What a feast! You can share,
Other sparrows are welcome and occasional thrush,
But watch out for next-door's cats, she has two.
I'm full, how about you?
We need to settle for the night,
You can share my branch and nest, if you like.
It's high, dry, cosy and warm,
Safe from our enemies, at least until dawn.
Another day, oh did you see that?
A tasty treat of bacon rind's been eaten by that tabby cat.

Sheila Neary

GARDEN RHYTHM

Sunday morning in the garden, half the world not yet awake,
I get busy with the planting, attack the soil with hoe and rake.
Vent the greenhouse, water seedlings, rescue hostas from the slugs,
Feed the fishes and the roses, slaughter half a million bugs.
Scatter seed and fill the birdbath, top up peanuts in their cage,
Only blackbirds at this hour, watch the squirrels fume and rage.

See the drops from last night's rainfall sparkle on the springtime leaves,
And in the compost heap, the wood mice steal away like
                                        night-time thieves.
Small butterflies invade the holly, a mist of blue to match the sky,
Whilst in the empty heavens above them, a plaintiff sound,
                                        a rook's lone cry.

Houses stirring, windows opening, people sliding from their beds,
Dogs are barking, children shouting, men go hiding in their sheds.
Sunday morning in the garden, now the world is wide awake,
Roar of mowers, blast of music, retreat indoors for coffee break.

Lucy Holloway

MY PRIZE BEAUTY

Geranium in bloom, what a colourful sight,
Scarlet and pink and one dazzling white.
But forlorn in a corner, neglected alone,
Stands a broken clay pot, its contents unknown.

Three woody steams stick out of the earth,
Lifeless they look, no sign of rebirth.
But as the sun's rays penetrate through the glass,
Healthy green shoots begin to amass.

One by one bell shaped flowers unfurl,
Gracefully swaying and doing a twirl.
I was so proud of my plant that had decided to grow,
I entered it in the flower show.

It didn't win, but it got third prize,
Well, the first and second - were double its size.
If my lovely fuchsia had only known,
That into the compost heap it had nearly been thrown.

Barbara Senior

LOVE, SPRING'S ETERNAL TOIL

The furrows strong, the furrows straight
There's a feeling that's not quite so great
As turning the earth upside down
Changing its colour from green to brown

To dig, to cultivate, to sow
With prayers and hopes to watch it grow
The cycle starts around again
With help from the Lord with sun and rain

Although we toil with aching back
Sometimes late frosts can set us back
It brings disappointment, sometimes a tear
But to the gardener there's always next year

Len Simms

STORMY WEATHER

The raindrop was a hurling stone
I was glad I was not alone
the wind pushed and screamed by
across the darkened night-time sky

The windows rumbled in their space
the roof heaved as if out of place
cold clung to the pre-dawn air
as the season made known 'I am here'

Then as if out of steam
the wind stopped its wicked scream
the rain came down gently now
as the wind took its final bow

Kareen Smith

SPRING

Down the valley
And across the lea,
Birds are a-flitting
Through each tree.
Cheeping and chirping,
Their hearts filled with glee.
The sun is shining
Spring has begun.
A robin sits on a leafy bough
Screeching at a fox, way below.
Sly old fox steals quietly by,
Not a sound, as on he glides.
A nice fat rabbit he's spied,
High in the sky, a hawk, sharp of eye.
Saw bunny below, so fat and round,
An easy meal he thought he'd found.
But wise old bunny just fled underground.

Doris Richards

AWAKENING

The blossoms on the cherry tree,
A murmuring from a passing bee,
Sweet butterfly in search of love,
The cooing of the collared dove,
Bright wallflowers' perfume drifting by,
Gay pansy with its cheeky eye,
All these things I hold most dear,
And soon the swallow will be here.

The ladybird awakes from sleep,
And starlings on the pea sticks cheep,
Two jackdaws chacking from the bough,
The distant mooing of a cow,
The sky above is blue and clear,
And soon the swallows will be here.

As primroses begin to fade,
Beneath the trees a different shade,
The bluebell with its wondrous hue,
Illuminates with violet blue,
Its haunting perfume fills the air,
And soon the swallows will be here.

Valerie Mellor

THE FOX

A fox went out on his daily run
Hoping to find his meal in the sun
He spied a rabbit but it was too quick
It ran so fast like a crack of a whip

He was so tired out after his quest
And thought he'd lay down awhile and take a rest
Then he heard the sound of a hunter's horn
And knew it was time for him to be gone

Away cross the fields he could hear the hounds bray
And thoughts of a meal were gone for the day
The sounds of the huntsmen became very clear
His heart beat much faster and he trembled with fear

He thought that his days were nearly done
Until hounds and hunters he'd outrun
Safe at last his lair he found
And another fox had gone to ground.

B P Willetts

SHEEP

I watched them, one by one,
Some seemed to wink at me.
Their dark and globulous eyes twitching
Like balls of crackling coal in dying fires.
Peering mischievously upon the rolling moor land
Of the wild Yorkshire Dales,
Sheepish smiles twisting over soot-black, lipless mouths,
Reclining idly on dunes of grass,
What were they thinking, those unhurried woollen snowballs?
Curdled clumps of clotted cream, what dreams spun seamlessly
Throughout the spindles of their minds?
In which language did they articulate
Their clustered thoughts and ponderings?
What melodies spooled softly among their memories?
Do they remember me, yet now?
Gently they grazed, languidly they moved,
Large tortoises in frocks of curling cloud,
Breathing in cool sunny air
In the spring of eighty-eight.
Where are they now?

Simon Zonenblick

GREEN

The fresh bright newness of leaves in spring
Newly mown grass before the summer drought
Green vegetation soft to the eye
Crisp crunch to the palate.
Salad slippery, smooth to the tongue.
Arching green foliage forming tunnels of dappled light
Creating happiness to the soul.
Walking in the sunshine, through new growth of green.
Dampness turning to mould
Green clinging onto gnarled bark
Lichen, moss, smelling of damp.
Tarnish on silver, shading reflection.
Jealousy, green monster clouding the mind.
The freshness of green, sublimated by pain
Longing to break out, to experience rebirth and the pleasure of green.

Gael Nash

WOODS OF THE ANCIENT ONES

Woods of the Ancient Ones I hear your song.
How I love to walk your pathways,
then to caress your old gnarled bark,
and remember distant days.

I feel the memories of old,
I look skyward to your canopy bare.
Your calm brings warmth each day,
your arms protect all who shelter there.

White softness covers your being,
bringing a velvety winter outline.
Shading my eyes against the glare,
I feel that it will soon be time.

I sigh and give thanks -
to this forest of winter waiting,
for soon spring will replenish you,
another years cycle will be arriving.

Josephine Carter

GAZEBOS IN GARDENS

Gazebos in gardens are perfect
To meditate and romance awhile
Embrace our emotions in wonder
Complete in fantasy and style

Gardens with treasures are special
Forever flowing in natural schemes
Early spring, summer, autumn, winter
Speak of nature's wondrous scenes

Tree pipits sing with pleasure
Musical notes with happy sounds
Dreams of clarity and unity
Magic thrilling moments abound

Daffodils in cascades of colour
Carpet the earth in pure delight
Dragonflies skim silently up river
Searching bees buss in flight

Elizabeth Hunter

BUTTERFLY

Butterfly, oh butterfly
With painted wings so bright
Your body glistens as you fly
Wings trembling in sheer delight
May your wholeness richly flourish
Through a system of your own
Flicker silently and nourish
From the seeds that nature has sown

Should you ever take a breath
Extracted from the breeze
Note - as in a treble clef -
The blackbird sings to please
Colours shine, two blinking fans
Which carry you around
Continue on, float patiently
Above the gentle ground

Butterfly, oh butterfly
Why do you aim so high?
Can you see the winding rivers
As you glide into the sky?
Some time it takes to travel round
Your form keeps quiet distance
Moments happen, without a sound
Then you are gone, *within an instant.*

Kathleen McCarthy

GYPSY GIRL

Gypsy girl with skirts of colours bright
Like a rainbow dancing in the light
Free to love, free to care, this gypsy girl is everywhere
She has a caravan to travel and roam
It's painted so fine, her cosy home
This girl loves the grass beneath her feet
To run through fields of golden wheat
Yes my Lord I hear her cry
I'm part of earth, of sun, of sky
She likes the scent of rain upon her face
To stand and feel all time and space
Watching a robin on that old wooden gate
A little rabbit hurrying, he must be so late
Blossom floating by like snowflakes in May
A happy girl on a sunny day
A woodland of bluebells they catch her eye
She carries them with her as she passes by
She adores singing and dancing with her tambourine
Flowing black hair, what a wonderful scene
Yes my Lord I can hear her cry
I'm part of earth, of sun, of sky
Gypsy

Beryl Barlow

THE WORLD ABOUT US

Rivers, streams, seas and oceans,
Waters that keep the world in motion.
The sun, moon and twinkling stars,
Keeping time in minutes and hours.
The frost, snow, wind and rain,
Cleaning up the world again.
Large and small animals and birds,
Bring sweet music to our ears.
A golden sun to warm the day -
Bright moonlight to show the way.
Seasons changing through the year,
New life growing everywhere.
Nature's gifts are free to you,
A panoramic scene to view!

Sheila Waller

KESTREL, AT SUNSET

He hovers on silver, shivers wingfuls
Of power out of his brown mantle, stern
And stone, eyes trained on the chasm of beach:

Watching from the cliff, I've rising brimfuls
Of devil in me too for joining in,
Beside the pilot of the dusk, in reach

Of gods - to join his vigil every time
He takes a new vantage, to press against
The pink-gold blur of the west, for the danced
Discovery - to dive, to veer, to chime

Kew, kew! - Weightless, I climb!

Chris White

COLOURS OF MONDAY

Monday came and quickly went,
A strange day really,
The sky was grey and the clouds kissed the trees,
Rain cleansed the Earth and oh my goodness, what a breeze!
For some the day may have been dull,
Really dull and really cold.
The sun played hide and seek in the sky,
The birds stayed hidden, not daring to fly.
A strange day, yes, I suppose it was,
People wandered looking lost.
A good day though to reflect and see,
If everything in life was as it should be.
The grass was still green and the trees stood true,
The sky changed to a deep hazy blue.
Flowers held their heads up high,
Flashing their colours to all that passed by.
So that day, I suppose, really proved,
All was the same, nothing had moved.
Some people were happy, others were sad,
Always the same, not because the weather was bad.
What a bright, happy day that Monday was,
For some everyday is dull, just because
Their eyes are closed and they cannot see,
What a wonderful place this world can be.
Strange days, yes, I suppose they are,
For those who are blinkered and cannot see far.

Sara Church

UNTITLED

There are gardens full of beauty,
Some overgrown with weeds.
Many have a fountain
And hollyhocks and trees.

There are gardens that have roses,
With bluebells in-between.
Little secret pathways
Where rabbits can be seen.

Tall foxgloves in dark places,
Lupins blue and white.
A garden where the lilies grow,
A haven filled with light.

A garden is a pleasure,
A wonder to behold,
Where every season blossoms,
New beauties to unfold.

Deana Sawyer

GARDEN GHOST

Spirit of creativity
You are my muse
Your hands cruise delicately
Through the garden of coolness and soothe.

Spiritualistic green fingers
Plant seeds so minute
Your loving touch can enable growth
Of a lily so beautiful and cute.

The inhabitants of your garden
Take it for granted
They will eventually destroy it
Even though it's their own planet.

Conor McGreevy

EARLY SPRING IN THE PARK

Now old ladies are coming out in hats,
fathers are pushing prams
and daring boys zoom on skateboards.
Little dogs of snow-white,
big dogs of bold black
freely dash about sniffing the eager smells.

Gardeners slowly digging up old growth
stop and chat to anyone passing,
then plant patterns of new blooms
in the beds of brown earth.
While in the nearby bushes bashful buds
peep out at them.

On the bleak canvas of faded green
dabs of warm pink and yellow flowers
are splashed capriciously.
Galaxies of daisies and dandelions star shine
to brighten up the dull grass
and make light the morning.

Around the duck pond,
sleeping in a cover of early mist,
golden hazes of long fingered willow glow.
And the dark lace silhouettes of trees
stretch their powerful branches
to touch the grey and blue skies.

In a bald branch a lone kingfisher sits hunched,
then swiftly skims along the muddy stream,
a glorious flash of startling hues,
a beacon of dancing colour,
only to be glimpsed on a day
tinged with magic.

Helen Dalgleish

DAYDREAMS OF MY ENGLISH ROSE

In a misty meadow by a flowing stream
I close my eyes and daydream
Sunbeams dancing on the waters lapping below
With a warm sparkling golden glow
With hills many shades of green
The birthplace of that tranquil stream
I slip deeper into my dream and feel the warm, fragrant misty breeze
Passing through the swaying trees
Then gently flowing with the rippling stream to the silvery seas
Bearing blue birds, honeybees and butterflies
Beneath those vast blue summer skies
Then in the misty meadow by the stream
I open my eyes and see my dream
My true love from all those years lost
An angel from Heaven like Genesis at my cost
With her warm, silent, tender, patient repose
At last I see my beautiful, beautiful English rose.

Keith Potter

WALLED GARDEN

A garden walled, secret and secure,
All that's within, fresh and pure.
A garden to wander in tranquillity,
Be at one with all, in deep serenity.

This garden serene, calming away stress,
Scent of flowers, sweet aromas bless.
Exotic plant blooms giving you cheer,
Waterfalls, fountains and pools deep and clear.

Golden carp swim, free in the sunlight,
Their bodies shimmering like stars in the night.
The sound of songbirds to greet out ears,
So beautiful, almost brings tears.

A place from everyday stress you can hide,
Here, sheltered from the world outside,
To walk lightly in a world of your own,
Collecting thoughts shared, you have known.

This garden is with you, wherever you go,
It's inside you deep, only for you to know.
You can go there, as and when you will,
Feel all stress and tension, out of you spill.

Alan J Morgan

BEYOND THE BREAKERS

Amid the harsh world of tides
lies the battleground of the hunters
and the hunted

Where the shore ends the creatures in the sea take over
yet we see little of their lives

Leisurely limpets cling to wave battered rocks
while mighty mussels anchor their hinged homes
close to their allies

Quarrelsome crabs camouflaged from predators
and slithering sea slugs storing stings
to fire at the enemy

Foraging fish dart furiously among the sea anemones
and greedy gulls hover overhead
screaming their scavenger cry, sensing the living larder below

But tranquil at dusk,
the shore is seemingly at peace,
as the rippling waves creep steadily in to make a strand line

All the senses at once set reeling
in appreciation of Mother Nature working overtime
to create a wondrous underwater world

Liz Jacques

SUMMER IS ALMOST HERE

The sun filters through the soft green leaves,
Something is stirring,
Birds are flitting from garden to garden,
In search of food for their young,
Sleeping buds have now awakened,
The garden has given birth.
What was once a barren patch
Has now produced an array of mixed blooms,
Daffodils and tulips have almost peaked,
Bluebells are in abundance,
Cornflowers and marigolds sway in the breeze,
The grass needs a cut and the conifer trees are overgrown,
Weeds make their daily appearance,
The weather's getting warmer,
Summer is almost here.

P Dowse

THE OLD MAN

Upon the wooden garden bench sits old Stan - a lonely man,
Looking at the garden tools, a spade, a fork, a watering can.
He remembers years ago, he was strong and gardening mad,
Now he thinks, I'm just too old, I'm weak and frail, it is so sad.
My garden looked so beautiful with flowers, trees and shrubs,
Hanging baskets in the porch, geraniums in tubs,
Blooms of many colours and roses climbing high,
It looked just like a rainbow had fallen from the sky.
Everyone admired it, the neighbours all looked in,
Now it looks so bare and bleak, it really is a sin.
He planted all his bulbs and seeds with tender loving care,
Now the garden's full of weeds - it's more than Stan can bear.
If I could get some help he thought, then I'd give it a try,
The neighbours used to talk to me, now they just pass by,
I sit upon my garden bench, feeling in despair,
Thinking of the days gone by, no one seems to care.
A little boy lived down the road; he could see my plight,
'I'll help you out old man,' he said, 'We both will make it right.'
I showed him how to dig and hoe and how to sew the seeds,
He was so keen and full of pride, he cleared up all the weeds.
His little hands worked willingly, I taught him all I know,
He planted flowers, shrubs and trees, now we can watch them grow.
My garden looks so beautiful, that gave them a surprise,
The neighbours now they stop and stare, they can't believe their eyes.
I sit and glance around me; my heart is full of joy,
He's all grown up, a gardener now, not just a little boy,
So here we sit upon the bench, there's two of us, not one,
And I'm not lonely anymore, I love him like a son.

Hilary Ambrose

A NEW BEGINNING

Just moved in two weeks ago
    And left the garden I did grow

Many hours I did spend
    Mail order plants I did send

My plot was packed to the brim
    Designed as not to let weeds in

But alas I've said goodbye
    As a teardrop filled my eye

My new place is very bare
    Neglected with no one to care

Daises and moss for a lawn
    Borders of nettles and hawthorn

So unloved to say the least
    This garden is in for such a feast

Armed with cuttings I did come
    I'll soon have those weeds on the run.

Tina Butterworth

WELCOME SPRING

Is that spring in the air?
Delicate white and green of snowdrops
Crocus big and blousy, like a patchwork quilt
Snakehead lilies put their heads above the grass
But beware the frost is still in the air

Was that the sun peeping through?
Is that the yellow of the daffodil?
Primroses out before their day
Bright polyanthus show the way
Open greenhouse for the day

The sun gets higher every day
Tulips are trying to say 'hello'
Curling their heads to catch some sun
Lambs frolicking in the fields
Sounds of the farmers working the land

The blackbird sings her song high in the apple tree
Wake up, wake up, spring is here
Behind us now winter gone
Exciting times ahead.

Teresa R Chester

SUMMER LOVING

A shower of white daises nodding welcome to the breeze
Crowds of excited bluebells dancing under trees
Mountaineering sweet pea blossoms covering its throne
Puddles of bright sunlight fall on rough hewn stone

Earth warm and safe under thick emerald sheets
Shrubs heavy limbed holding red berry sweets
Oak stands, proud father, with benevolent gaze
Honeysuckle on fence tops and trellis will laze

Around all this the insects merrily chase
As summer enfolds them in loving embrace.

S Ballard

WEED SHALL SURRENDER

Right, you're for it now,
Rolling up my sleeves,
Ready for the fight of my life,
I pushed and pulled,
Grunted and groaned.

Falling to the floor,
Defeated,
I gave up hope,
All that effort for nothing,

Sat there mocking me,
The weed hadn't budged an inch.

Clare Stubbs

WORLD FROM NATURE'S WINDOW

Hear the lovely birds soothing serenade,
And the silent movers pass,
Being alone by choice, yet instruction,
Underneath the pure sapphire sky.
An unattended landscape through the window,
Cluttered with youth's activity,
Animals' habitat, a lush supply.
Of grotty changing splendour,
Peep through the delicate mesh,
Set eager eyes upon opulent nature,
Pearl-white lilies open like deep horizon,
And plum heather blossoms scattering along a boundless path,
Like my own sturdy superiors,
Three wise, matured trees bulky with life, spirit a vague vitality,
Overlook my rest place granting unseen content.
Waving guidance in the eastern breeze,
Neat black pots placed as regular as sunrise,
Upon tedious, orderly sectioned ground
With voluptuous leaves and blush flowers,
Rarely seeked for pleasure or satisfaction.
Small, soft stripes of cloud lay dispersing,
An uneven pattern in the absence of life,
A series of transparent panes reflecting light from,
A marvellous thriving indicator, a dripping sliced orange,
                                     intuitive energy,
For a hungry mass of consuming creatures.

Hayley Slade

WE ARE STRANGERS

Here, my memory nearly emptied,
The heart of the poor people
bleeds to fill my soul.

And there . . . my night long as darkness,
My stars without motherhood and breasts.
As far as the sky, my moon cries
that we are strangers.

Here, I am abroad, but there,
My existence is dissolution.
So where am I? From a world
that's deaf to proclamation?
So where am I? From a civilisation
that kills without a shame,
whose truth dissolves?

My dreams are trampled her, here
my wishes linger there.
Alone each falling tear flees from its eyes.
So where am I?
Fleeing from the history of equality, sadness
the negation of the weakling,
fleeing from the time of servility
from the goods of slaves . . .

We are here, searching air for meaning.
Here, self same to set sail with the
breezes of lovers

Yet remain strangers.

Mekhled Al-zaza

THE SCARECROW

He stands menacing, in the vegetable plot
Keeping a careful watch over the old man's pride and joy

The polka dot planting of the summer beds
Looking collectively curious under the clear blue sky

He sees all, and he knows when the breeze comes and goes
The soft, gentle rain will patter down on his clothes

Quenching the thirst of the growing seeds
Making them grow for the old man's needs

Carrot, onion, cabbage and such
Will be tasty and wholesome when he's grown quite a bunch

The soft, precious soil is dusted off lovingly
Then he takes them inside to prepare for his tea

The shabby old scarecrow, his clothes are faded with the sun
Gets put back into the potting shed, his work is now done

Next year the old man will make him a hat
To keep off the rain as it runs down the path

He'll put him by the veggie plot, next to the crab apple tree
Then he'll again grow carrot, onion and cabbage for his tea

Sue James

A SINGLE SILENT FLAME

There in the distance shines a single silent flame
dancing in the darkness, yet you do not know its name
sometimes you think you see it, turn around but then it's gone
it's always there at sunset, right through to early morn

Your heart is where it touches you
glowing for all to see
but when it is extinguished
it's a painful place to be

the flame of love burns brightly
a love you cannot tame
I do not take it lightly
For love spells out your name

no matter what the distance
no matter where you are
my heart will be forever yours
be you near or far

The single silent flame is love
it burns brightly for you and I
I wondered how the flame burned bright
I now know the reason why

My reason is to be with you
To shine upon your heart
Forever I give my love so true
let us never be apart

Together we will watch it burn
enduring day by day
the flame of love will burn forever
and will never fade away

James I Robson